—WEAPONS OF THE— AMERICAN CIVIL WAR

WEAPONS OF THE AMERICAN CIVIL WAR

IAN V. HOGG

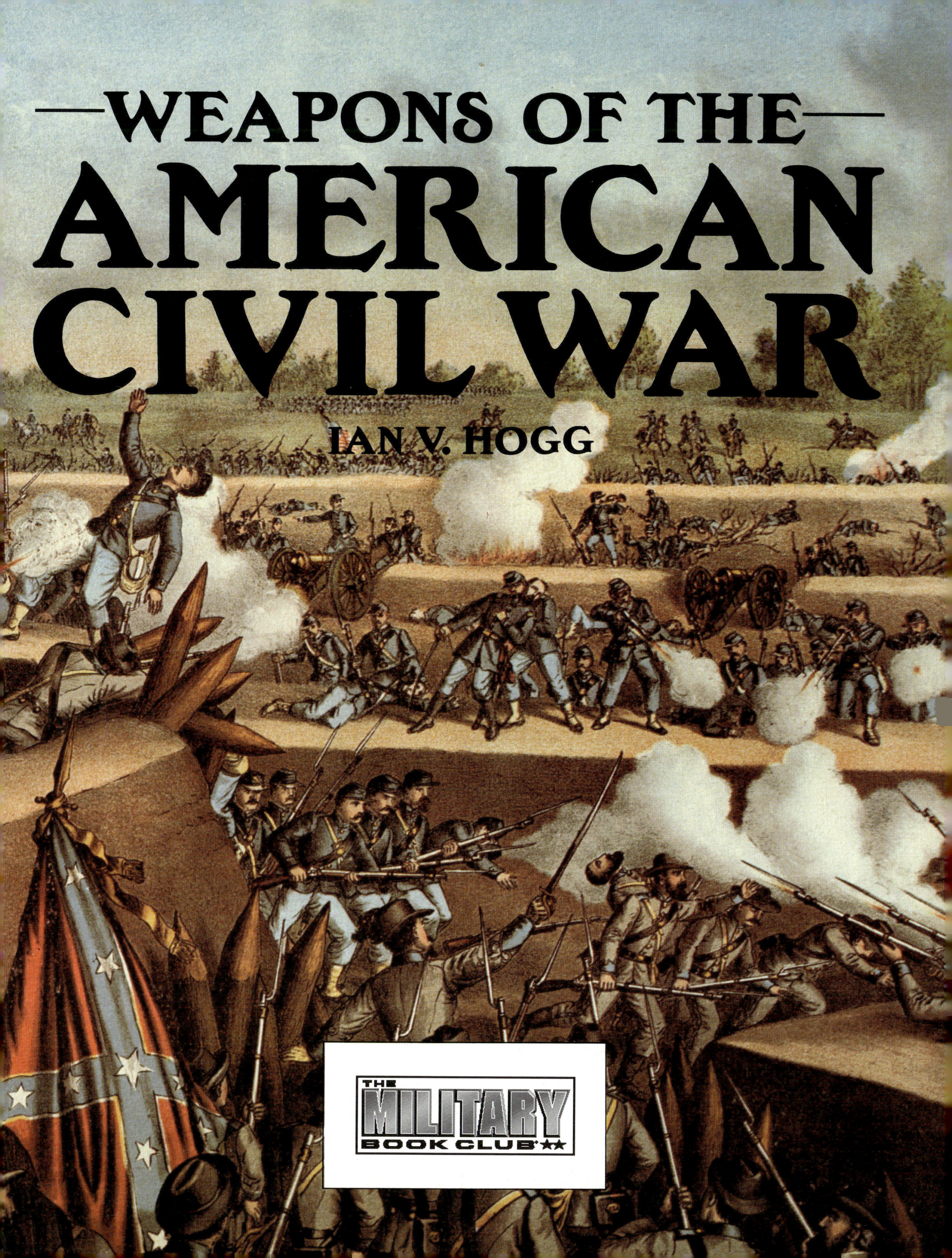

THE MILITARY BOOK CLUB

Published by
PRC Publishing Ltd
Kiln House
210 New Kings Rd
London SW6 4NZ

ISBN 1-85585-018-4

Printed in China

This edition published 1998 for
Parkgate Books Ltd.

Page 1: A Confederate artillery man poses beside his field gun.

Pages 2-3: Union troops storm the defenses of Petersburg.

This page: Men of the 26th New York Infantry on parade.

CONTENTS

1
THE CAVALRY AND ITS WEAPONS

Previous page: A confused engagement of cavalry and infantry during the Battle of the Wilderness, May 1864.

According to the old joke, the purpose of cavalry in warfare is to give tone to what would otherwise be an unseemly brawl. This may very well have been the case in Europe, but the cavalry of the Civil War was far removed from this image of 'elegant extras' parading in flamboyant uniforms. It was the principal shock element of the armies, and the exploits of this tough cavalry served as object lessons for armies throughout the world for many years; Jackson's campaign in the Shenandoah Valley, for example, was studied and restudied in staff colleges in Europe well into the first half of the twentieth century as an example of how mobile warfare should be conducted.

The value of cavalry can be estimated from their number. The Union eventually had 258 cavalry regiments, plus a further 170 independent cavalry companies, while the Confederate Army of North Virginia mustered four cavalry divisions made up of six brigades each holding an average of four regiments. This total, though, took time to accumulate; it also took time to train, and, above all else, it took time for the respective commanders to understand how best to employ their cavalry.

The Confederate Army had the best of the bargain for the first half of the war, largely because of the nature of the Southern society. There was a considerable leavening of gentry who were accustomed to riding and hunting, and even the farmers and laborers, due to the mainly agricultural nature of the area and its lack of other types of communication, were familiar with horse management and riding. The Union recruit, on the other hand, may have been familiar with horse management, but it was mainly as a beast of burden rather than as a mount.

In addition to this affinity for the horse, the Confederates seem to have grasped the purpose of cavalry more surely; a shock weapon, it needed to be handled in large bodies in order to make sure that it had some effect and was not frittered away in small handfuls. As a scouting force, to report back movements of the enemy, small groups of well-mounted men were essential; but as an arm of decision on the battlefield cavalry needed to be used in numbers.

Not that numbers alone could be decisive; against trained troops, cavalry beats in vain. But in most cases the troops in the first year or two of

Below: The headquarters staff of General Patrick, Union Army, pose for posterity at Bealton, Virginia, in 1863, with a fine collection of regulation swords.

Above: Lieutenant Colonel Hart, Assistant Adjutant-General of 3rd Union Corps, at Brandy Station, Virginia, February 1864, showing the saddlery and sidearms expected of officers at that period.

the war were not trained to anything like the standard necessary to withstand cavalry, and the first sign of a cloud of horse thundering towards them soon scattered all but the bravest, on either side. Given the combination of indifferent troops and a mass of cavalry, the odds are with the horsemen every time, and this fact was rapidly appreciated by the Confederate commanders, less rapidly by the Union, which persisted in using horse in 'penny packets' until late in 1863. In addition to being parcelled out for operations, the Union cavalry seems to have been an unwilling labor pool, raided to provide escorts for convoys, guards for headquarters, escorts for generals and a form of military police and occupation force for captured towns. Belatedly, probably as a result of studying Confederate use, the Union began to bring its cavalry together and form it into divisions and then into brigades, maneuvering it in larger tactical bodies. Once this took effect the quality of the Union cavalry began to improve, so that by mid-1864 the Union cavalry was the equal of the best of the Confederate force and soon surpassed them.

At the same time, the quality and effectiveness of the Confederate cavalry began to sink, largely due to attrition. The principal cause was the short-sighted Confederate system of demanding that every cavalryman provide his own horse. This was a highly effective way of building up a cavalry arm from nothing. Cavalry has always (rightly or wrongly) been considered as an élite body, and once war broke out many Confederate men came forward dragging a horse behind them, safe in the knowledge that provision of a horse would ensure them a place in the cavalry and thus safeguard them from the indignity of becoming foot soldiers. They were paid a small allowance for the 'hire' of the horse, and should it be killed during a battle they were reimbursed at its valuation on enlistment. But if the animal merely succumbed to the rigors of campaigning, the owner got nothing. And as the war went on horses became more scarce and more expensive, so that a dismounted cavalryman could not afford to replace his mount and was remustered into the infantry. In this way the numbers of cavalry slowly dwindled.

Left: Major Albert G Enos, 8th Pennsylvania Cavalry, wearing a double-breasted 'Mounted Officer's Jacket' and carrying a heavy cavalry saber.

Swords

The cavalry, of whichever side, was always armed with three weapons – the sword, the carbine and the pistol. The traditional cavalry weapon was, of course, the saber, a sword with a thick back edge to give it strength when used in a sweeping blow from a speeding horse. In Union service sabers were divided into two classes, light and heavy. The light cavalry saber Model 1860 had a 41-inch blade, one inch wide at the hilt, which was slightly curved. The guard was of brass in half-basket form, the grip was covered in black leather bound with brass wire, and the pommel was in the shape of a Phrygian helmet. The heavy cavalry saber Model 1840 was similar but had a slightly thicker blade, one and a quarter inches deep at the hilt. Both used a plain wrought-iron scabbard with two suspension rings for attachment to the belt. During the war the Union purchased 203,285 light and 189,114 heavy sabers.

The Confederate cavalry used swords which were little more than copies of the Union patterns but of generally poorer finish. The blades were not so well finished, the grips were wrapped in oiled cloth or brown leather secured by copper, brass or iron wire. The guards were roughly made from cast or wrought brass. In addition numbers of foreign swords appeared; the British Pattern 1853 cavalry saber was often seen in Confederate hands, while non-regulation designs were bought from German swordsmiths.

Some Confederate cavalry carried lances, particularly state volunteer forces in the early part of the war. These were generally an eight-foot ash staff carrying a 10-inch spear tip just under two inches wide. The other end was shod with an iron ferrule, and there would be a leather wrist-loop about halfway along the staff. Pennons were carried by some formations, below the spear tip. But as the war progressed it soon became apparent that the lance was a somewhat useless weapon, and by early 1863 its use had been abandoned except by rear-area defense units which carried lances largely for show.

The reason for the abolition of the lance was simply that the function of cavalry was undergoing change. Even though they were still shock troops, capable of mounting a fearsome charge, more of their work became that of mounted infantry; they would use their horses to reach a point of contact and then dismount to fight on foot before remounting to take up pursuit or conduct a fighting withdrawal. As a result the carbine became a far more useful and important weapon than the lance.

Below: Union cavalry charge into battle at Cedar Creek, October 1864.

Carbines

The carbine, by definition, is a short and light version of the standard rifle. In fact, and in the Civil War, it frequently bore little or no relationship to the infantryman's weapon. The 1860s were a time of innovation in firearms and many carbine designs were never seen as long rifles.

The official Union cavalry carbine was the US Pistol Carbine Model 1855, which was no more than the standard Model 1855 single-shot .58 caliber pistol with a long barrel and a separate shoulder stock which could be attached when required. Normally the pistol was carried in a saddle holster and used one-handed, but when precision was called for, or dismounted action, then the stock was removed from another holster, attached to the butt, and the weapon then used as a carbine. This, though, was a pre-war weapon of which only 8000 had ever been made, and it was found only in regular units.

The Union volunteer forces had some freedom of choice in the selection of arms, and most of the cavalry regiments opted for the Spencer carbine. The Spencer was one of the few carbine designs which echoed a longer rifle, and it was simply a shorter model of the Spencer infantry rifle, although almost ten times as many carbines were purchased as rifles.

The Spencer is generally considered to be the first successful repeating rifle, and its success was due to the fact that it used a self-contained metallic cartridge. A tube containing seven cartridges was inserted through a trapdoor in the butt, and a spring in this tube forced the cartridges forward. A lever, forming the trigger guard, was forced down; this swung the breech block back and down until the first cartridge in the tube was able to slide into a recess in the top of the block. Returning the lever now forced this cartridge into the chamber and closed the breech. A separate hammer was cocked, the trigger pulled, and the hammer descended on to a firing pin which fired the cartridge. Operating the lever again first extracted and ejected the spent case, then reloaded the next round.

The remarkable thing about the Spencer was that it had been invented by a 20-year-old youth, Christopher M Spencer, who, early in the Civil War, appeared in Washington with a prototype

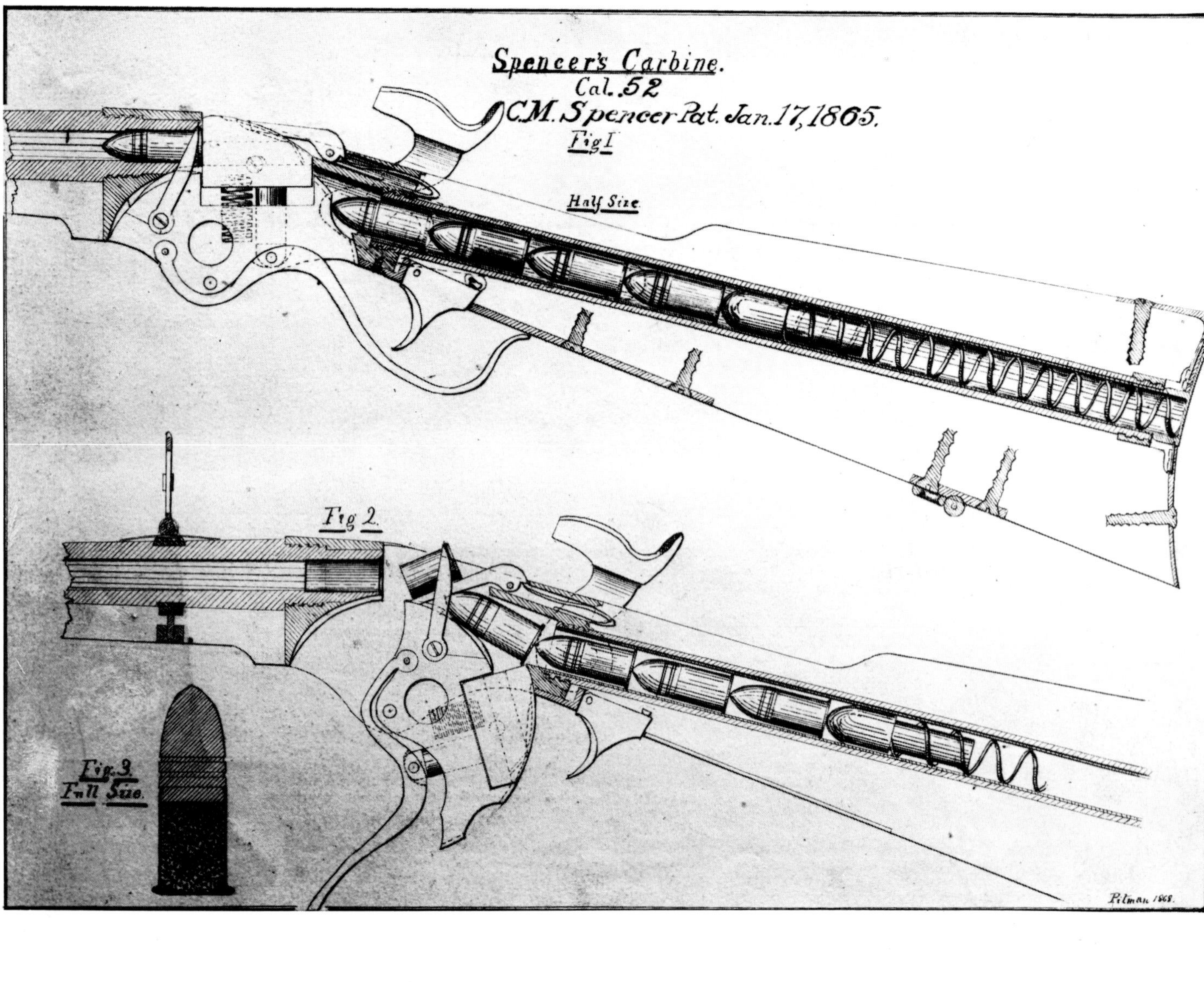

Below: An extract from the patent drawings of Spencer's carbine, showing the method of ammunition supply through the butt and the operation of the breech block.

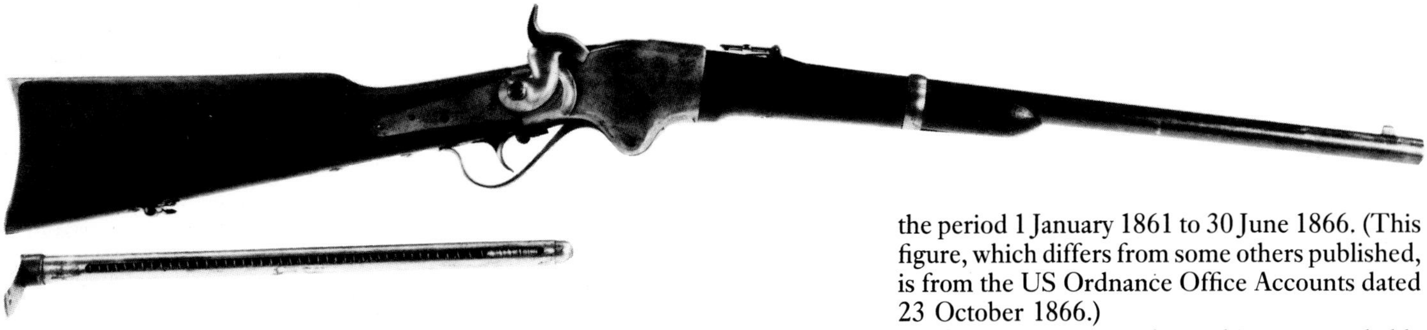

Above: A Spencer Carbine, showing the spring-loaded magazine removed from the butt.

gun hoping to obtain a contract. Since Washington was then full of men attempting to sell guns of every shape and size, nobody took much notice of this beardless youth. Eventually, almost at the end of his patience, he managed to gain an audience with President Lincoln. Lincoln listened, then invited the boy to come outside into the grounds of the White House and demonstrate the gun. This he did. Lincoln then tried it, was impressed, and from that came an order from the Navy department for a specimen for test in June 1861. The War Department followed with its own tests later in the year, but turned the Spencer down. In a letter to the Secretary of War in December 1861 the Chief of Ordnance, Brigadier-General Ripley, said:

> The reports heretofore made are favorable so far as the limited trials went, but they do not go farther than to suggest or recommend the procurement of a sufficient number to place in the hands of troops in the field for trial . . . I regard the weight of the arm, with the loaded magazine, as objectionable, and also the requirement of a special ammunition rendering it impossible to use the arms with ordinary cartridges or with powder and ball. I do not discover any important advantage of these arms over several other breech-loaders . . .
>
> In view of the foregoing, of the very high prices asked for these arms, and of the fact that the Government is already pledged on orders and contracts for nearly 73,000 breech-loading rifles and carbines, to the amount of two and a quarter million dollars, I do not consider it advisable to entertain either of the propositions for purchasing these arms.

The fact, though, was that the Spencer was far better than most other weapons of the day, and whether or not an official contract was forthcoming, several regiments decided to acquire it privately. The first recorded use of the Spencer was in June 1863, in the hands of Wilder's Mounted Brigade at Hoover's Gap and in the Tullahoma campaign. The Government had, by then, relented and begun official purchasing, and the first official Spencer carbines were issued to the Michigan Cavalry Brigade in January 1863, being used by them at the Battle of Gettysburg. A total of 94,196 Spencer carbines, to the value of $2,393,633.82 were purchased by the Union in the period 1 January 1861 to 30 June 1866. (This figure, which differs from some others published, is from the US Ordnance Office Accounts dated 23 October 1866.)

The next most popular carbine was probably the Sharps Model of 1859 or the later Model 1863. The Sharps gained an extremely high reputation for accuracy – the nickname 'Sharpshooter' came not from any sharpness of aim, but from the fact that the Sharps could turn average shots into crack shots if they wished, and Colonel Hiram Berdan's 'Sharpshooters' were entirely armed with this weapon.

The Sharps was one of the earliest, strongest and most successful breech-loading weapons. Christian Sharps took out his patents in 1848, and his original designs were for a weapon firing a paper cartridge with separate percussion cap. A lever forming the trigger-guard was forced down; this caused the solid steel breech block to slide downwards in guides, exposing the rear end of the chamber. A paper cartridge, carrying the powder and ball, was inserted into the chamber and the block was closed; as it moved up to close, so the sharp edge of the block sheared off the paper at the rear of the cartridge, exposing the powder within. A nipple on the block was now crowned with a percussion cap and the trigger pulled to drop a hammer on the cap. The flame passed through a vent in the block and ignited the powder in the chamber. On opening the breech there was, of course, nothing in the chamber to extract. Most of the early Sharps weapons were provided with ramrods so that when powder fouling built up, as it inevitably did, and the breech became stiff and difficult to operate, it could be muzzle loaded in the traditional manner until the opportunity for cleaning presented itself. Like the Spencer, the Sharps was of .52 caliber; the M1859 was distinguished by having brass barrel bands and furniture, whereas the M1863 used iron for the various external components. A total of 80,512 Sharps carbines, to the value of $2,213,192, were purchased by the Union authorities.

The Burnside carbine was invented by General Ambrose E Burnside, who had retired from the Union Army in 1853 and set up the Burnside Arms Company in 1855. In 1856 he patented his breech-loading single-shot carbine which used a special brass cartridge of his own design. This was a conical brass case containing black powder and with a bullet fixed in the front end, but the rear carried no means of ignition, merely a hole through which the flame from an external percussion cap passed. The breech block of the

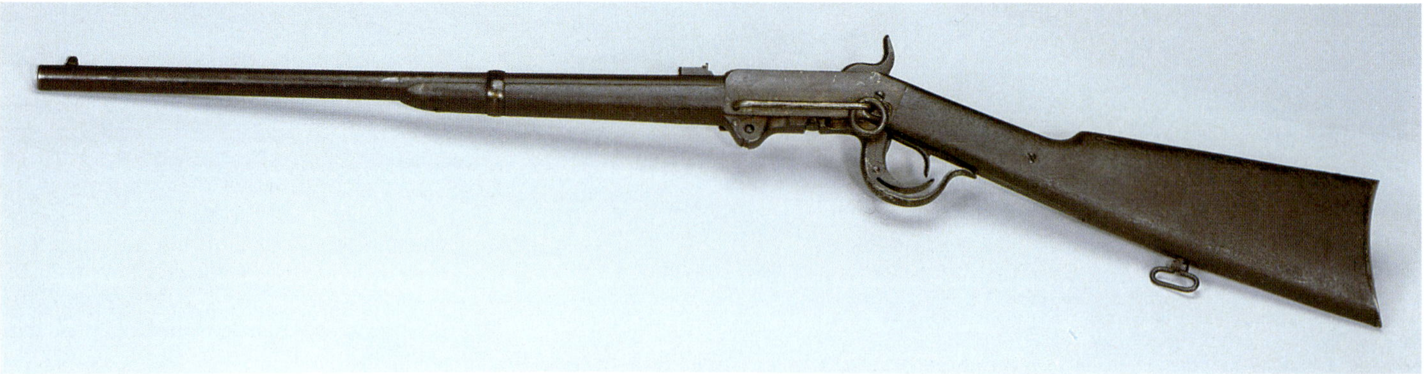

Above: A .54 caliber Model 1864 Burnside carbine.

Below: Two detail views of a Burnside carbine with the hammer cocked exposing the position for the percussion cap and the breech in the open position.

Burnside contained the chamber, a vent and a cap nipple, and was hinged to the rear end of the barrel, inside the gun's frame. Operating the usual trigger-guard lever allowed this block to be swung down into a vertical position, exposing the mouth of the chamber. The cartridge was dropped base-first into the chamber and the block was closed, aligning the chambered cartridge with the barrel. A cap was then placed on the nipple, and it was struck by the usual external hammer.

The Burnside was reliable and quite accurate; at a test carried out in Washington Navy Yard in 1859 a specimen Burnside carbine fired 500 shots in succession without cleaning and without misfire. These were all aimed shots, fired at a target 500 yards away, and of the 500 bullets only 60 missed the target – a figure which included 30 which had been blazed off without particular aim in order to determine the maximum rate of fire. A report from the western plains averred that a buffalo had been killed at 800 yards' range by one shot from a Burnside.

As might be imagined, Burnside was called back to active duty when the war began, being appointed Major-General of Volunteers, and by all accounts was a good leader who acquitted himself well. His connections in the Army no doubt facilitated his carbine getting a hearing even before war broke out, and altogether 55,567 carbines worth $1,412,620.41 were purchased, together with 21,819,200 cartridges worth another $547,490.05.

Taken in order of quantity purchased, the Smith carbine, with 30,062 bought during the war, is the next most important Union design. This was the design of Gilbert Smith and was manufactured by the American Arms Company of Chicopee Falls, Massachusetts. The Smith was a top-break design, rather in the manner of a shotgun, opened by pressing in a catch just in front of the trigger. This broke the action just in front of the chamber, so that the cartridge could be loaded base-first into the chamber and the gun then closed. A percussion cap was placed on a nipple and fired by a hammer, and the flame passed through a vent, into the chamber, and fired the cartridge by passing through a hole in the base in a similar manner to the Burnside.

Some 300 Smith carbines were bought in 1860 for extended trial, though it appears probable that these were in the odd caliber of .56. The remainder of the 30,000 bought during the war were of the more usual .52 caliber.

The Starr carbine used a peculiar two-part breech block; operating the trigger-guard lever by swinging it down first slid a part of the block downwards to unlock the breech, then pivoted the rest backwards to expose the chamber. It was perhaps less complicated than it sounds, and it certainly made a strong breech joint. It used a linen cartridge and conical bullet, which was loaded into the chamber and the breech then closed. A cap was placed on the nipple on the upper breech block and firing was by an external

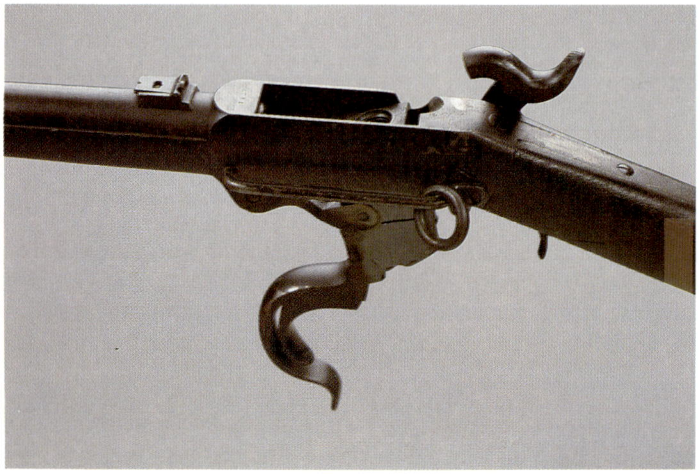

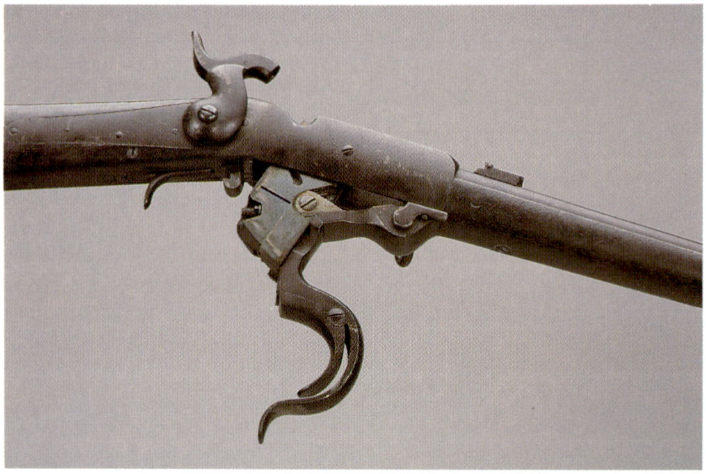

Above: Sharp's breech-loading carbine.

Below: The .52 caliber Starr carbine.

Bottom left: The Starr carbine with the breech partly open.

Bottom right: Top view of the Starr carbine, showing how the breech block pivots back so as to expose the chamber for loading.

hammer. A total of 25,603 Starr carbines was purchased.

Close on the heels of the Starr came the Gallagher carbine. This broke open halfway along the chamber, a system claimed to give easier extraction of the special brass cartridge, and the opening was done by the usual sort of trigger-guard lever. Pushing this down forced the barrel forward in the fore end, so as to move it away from the rest of the chamber, and then allowed it to swing down, exposing the rear end of the barrel and the forward half of the chamber. The cartridge, consisting of a paper-covered brass tube and a bullet, was inserted into the forward part of the chamber, and the gun was then closed. The closing action first swung down the rear end of the barrel and then drew it back into the frame so that the rear end of the cartridge entered the chamber. In fact it seems, from contemporary accounts, that the Gallagher could be loaded equally well by putting the cartridge base-first into the rear half of the chamber and then closing the gun. After that the usual hammer, cap and nipple came into play and the flame from the cap went through a hole in the base of the cartridge to fire the powder. A slight drawback appears to have been the rather long and tortuous vent, which soon clogged with fouling, but apart from this there were few complaints about the Gallagher's reliability. Some 22,000 were purchased.

The Maynard carbine was invented by a dentist, Dr Edward Maynard of Washington DC. In 1845 he had invented the 'Maynard Tape Priming' system in which pellets of detonating composition were spaced along a paper or linen tape. This tape was coiled inside a magazine in the stock of a weapon, and, by a ratchet device, was fed forward every time the hammer was cocked. This forward movement placed a pellet of composition on top of the usual sort of percussion nipple, so that when the trigger was pulled the hammer fell and fired it. Then, as the hammer

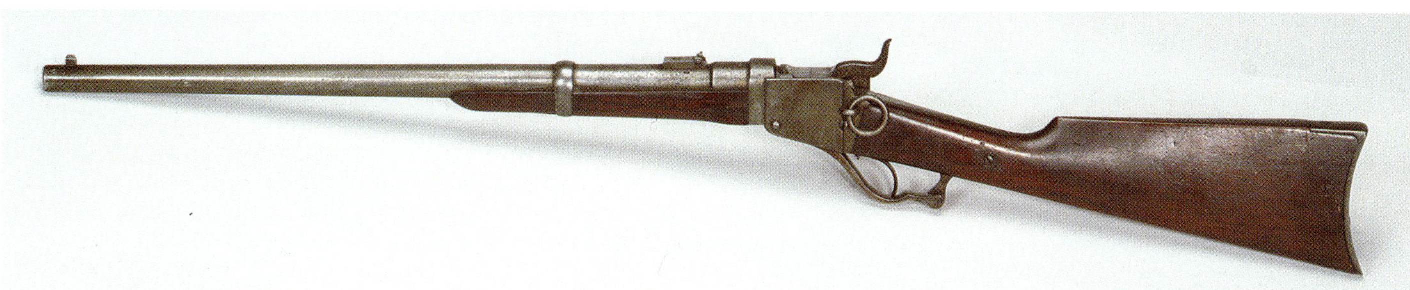

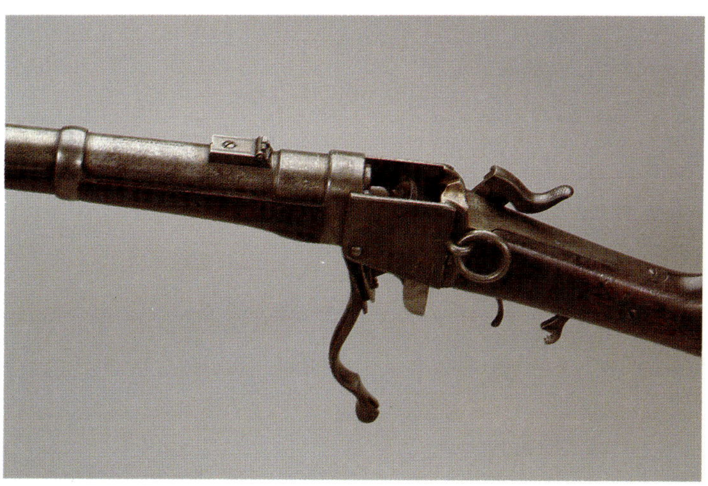

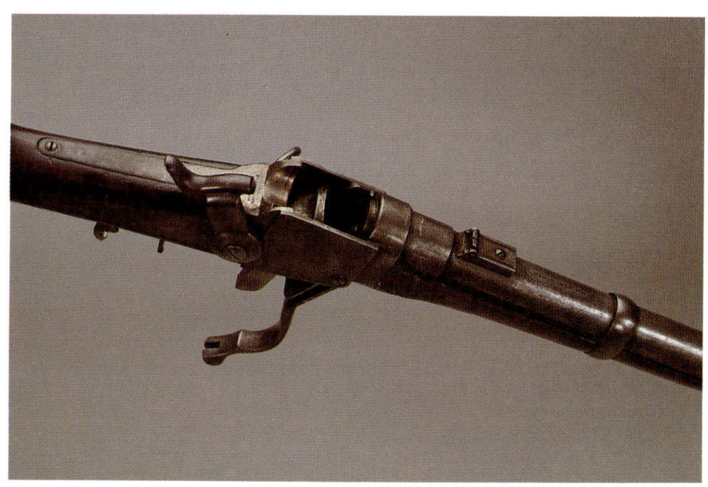

was pulled back, the mechanism placed another pellet on the nipple ready for the next shot. What Maynard invented is still with us today in the average child's cap pistol, though with rather less power.

Maynard's tape priming system was, of course, invented with muzzle-loading weapons in view, but in the 1850s, as breech loading began to appear, Maynard was quick to patent a breech-loading metallic cartridge with a hole in the base. He then followed this up with a suitable weapon, a carbine in .52 or .36 caliber in which a catch in the trigger-guard released the break-open action. The cartridge was inserted, the action closed and the hammer cocked, which, of course, pushed a pellet of priming onto the nipple. The official version used a priming tape with 60 pellets.

The Maynard was quite accurate. On test at the Navy Yard in 1859 it achieved a 100 percent hit rate with 250 shots fired at 500 yards' range, 80 percent of the shots falling within a four-foot square. At a range of 1300 yards 14 out of 43 shots struck a target 10 feet high and 30 feet wide, and, moreover, passed through the one-inch pine boards of which the target was built.

One feature of these breech-loaders using metallic cases with holes in the base was that, after firing, the cases could be cleaned and re-loaded, so long as the man had some powder and bullets. There is a report, also from the Washington Navy Yard, of two Maynard brass cases which had fired 100 rounds each and were still serviceable. Over two million Maynard cartridges were bought during the war, to accompany the 20,002 carbines purchased.

The Joslyn carbine, of which about 11,000 were purchased, was a deceptively simple design. The breech mechanism consisted merely of a hinged semi-cylindrical cap which dropped over the back end of the chamber to close it. The rear face of the swinging cover carried a nipple, and the gun was loaded with a linen cartridge and the nipple then capped. Reports on the efficiency of the Joslyn are hard to come by, but it is difficult to resist the conclusion that the breech sealing would have left a lot to be desired. It is notable

Below: Patent drawing of Joslyn's carbine. The breech closing plug has a gutta-percha sealing collar, a device which did not last long under arduous service.

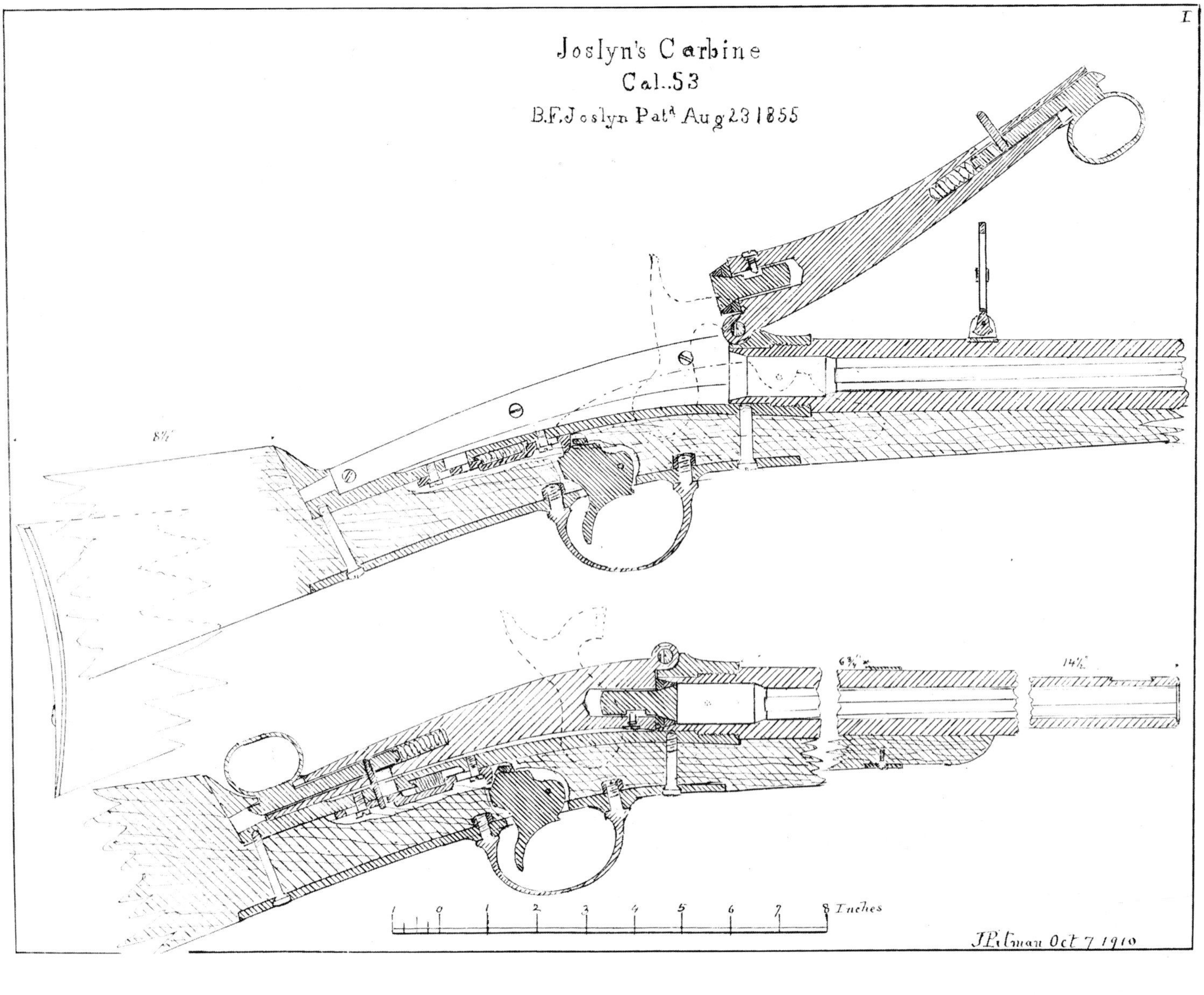

Above: The Remington 'Split Breech' carbine, fore-runner of the more famous 'Rolling Block' weapons, was supplied to Union forces in small numbers just before the Civil War ended. It fired a .50 rimfire cartridge.

that in postwar years almost all these Joslyn weapons were converted to use rimfire metallic cartridges.

In addition to these designs bought in some quantity, there were a number of less well-known carbines purchased in small numbers, largely to make up a shortfall at various times. Most of these were fairly simple break-open, single-shot weapons firing linen or paper cartridges from percussion caps. One interesting type is the Frank Wesson carbine, manufactured by the B Kitteredge Company of Cincinnati. This was a breech-loader with a 24-inch barrel using a .44 rimfire cartridge, and it is unusual in having two triggers and trigger-guards. In fact the forward trigger is the release which allows the barrel to be broken open, hinging down to expose the breech for loading. An external hammer was cocked and the gun closed, and the rear trigger was then used to release the hammer. On opening the carbine to unload the empty case, there was no form of built-in extractor, but the sides of the breech were cut away to allow the firer to grasp the case with his fingers and pull it out. Invariably, of course, the case was hot and well expanded, and resort to the ramrod was usual. Only 151 of these were ever purchased officially, by the Union Army shortly after Gettysburg, but many more were sold to militia units in nearby states. The commanding officer of the 1st Kansas Cavalry was so enthusiastic about the accuracy of the Wesson carbine that he happily furnished Kitteredge & Co with a signed testimonial.

The Confederate cavalry also armed themselves with carbines, though they had rather less choice than had the Union. For the sake of standardization the Army decided in 1863 to set up manufacture of the English Enfield Pattern '54 carbine, which was little more than a shorter version of the rifle of the same year. This was a simple percussion-cap-fired muzzle-loader, which was probably why it was selected, and a factory for its manufacture was set up in Alabama. It took time to get the factory organized, install the machinery and train the workforce, and it was not until April 1865 that the first batch of 900 carbines was delivered, by which time there was little point in continuing.

Other muzzle-loading carbines were manufactured by small gunmakers, simply copying either the Enfield or the US regulation Model 1854. Purchasing agents scoured Europe to buy up whatever they could, and the Richmond Armory produced a quite serviceable weapon by simply shortening their standard rifle musket.

One of the more common carbines was the Cook & Brother musketoon; this was a copy of the Enfield design, manufactured by two Englishmen named Cook at a small plant in New Orleans. With the approach of the Union Army to New Orleans they closed down their operation and moved the plant to Athens, Georgia, where they set up once more and eventually produced several thousand carbines and rifles.

Another copy weapon was the Hodgkins & Sons percussion carbine, though no more than about one hundred were made at their Macon, Georgia, factory in 1862-63. It was basically a short-barreled copy of the US Springfield M1855 musket, having a 22-inch barrel in .58 caliber.

Breech-loading carbines were prized by the Confederates, but there were few facilities for manufacturing them in the Southern states and consequently most of those in the hands of Confederates got there by being taken in battle. The drawback to this was, of course, that many of them needed special types of ammunition, and unless a supply of this could be captured as well there was not a great deal of point in having the weapon. But as early as 1862 the S C Robinson Arms Factory of Richmond set about manufacturing a copy of the Sharps carbine; after making just over 1800 of them the factory was taken over by the Confederate government in 1863 and production continued, another 3500 or so being made by the war's end.

Perhaps the most interesting Confederate carbine was the Morse, which was produced mainly for use by the South Carolina State Militia, though some weapons were acquired by other CSA troops. The significant feature of the Morse was that it used one of the first center-fire metallic cartridges ever devised. A breech-loader, the mechanism was very simply a block behind the chamber, carrying a firing pin, which could be withdrawn by operating a hinged lever lying across the top of the breech. Lifting this up and back moved the breech block straight back, so exposing the chamber for loading. The rimmed brass case, complete with bullet, was inserted, the block closed and the external hammer released by pressing the trigger. The firing pin then struck a percussion cap carried in a rubber ring in the base of the brass case. On opening the breech, the empty case was extracted and the gun reloaded. By removing the spent cap from the case and repriming it, inserting new powder and a bullet, the Morse case could be reused several times.

The Morse has a most interesting history. It was developed in the 1850s for the US Army and was submitted for trials in 1857. The US Army was impressed by the Morse system and in 1858 converted 54 Springfield .69 caliber muskets into this method of operation for trial. This proved successful and machinery was installed at Harper's Ferry Armory with the intention of converting all the US rifles and carbines to the Morse system. Then came the war, and the raid on Harper's Ferry, and the Confederates carried off much of the machinery which had been intended for carrying out the Morse conversions. This machinery was duly sent down to the factory of H Marshall & Co in Atlanta, Georgia, where it went to work manufacturing Morse carbines. Morse had thrown in his lot with the Confederates and had been appointed Superintendent of the Nashville Armory in 1861. But in 1862 he moved to Atlanta and took charge of the manufacture of the Morse carbine there. Upon the contract for supplying the South Carolina Militia, however, the machinery was moved from Atlanta to the State Military Factory in Greenville, South Carolina, and the majority of the thousand or so Confederate Morse carbines were made there. The products of the two manufactories can be distinguished; the Atlanta carbines have a long tail extension on the wooden fore end which extends all the way back to the trigger, while those made in Greenville have a brass plate behind the curtailed fore end.

The Morse carbine was by no means perfect; in its original form the brass breech block tended to set back under firing pressure, and the percussion caps, devoid of rear support, had a tendency to burst on firing and erode the face of the breech. Morse attempted to cure this by making a large, flanged iron firing pin which was supposed to protect the face of the breech, but eventually he changed the material of the breech block to iron and shaped it so that any gas leaking from the breech would be deflected forward, away from the firer's eye. All of which suggests that the Morse cartridge was not sealing the rear of the chamber very well.

Another original Southern design is the Tarpley carbine, of which a few hundred were made in 1863-64. This was invented by J H Tarpley of Greensboro, North Carolina, and was duly granted a Confederate patent (which in itself must be a rare distinction) in 1863. Manufacture was carried out by the J & F Garrett Company in Greensboro. The Tarpley used a vertical-sliding block breech, similar in general principle to that of the Sharps, but operated by a separate catch instead of by a trigger-guard lever. As with the Sharps, the final closing movement of the mechanism nipped off the end of the paper cartridge, and firing was done by a percussion cap fitted to a nipple on the block.

It might be added that there was a strong body of opinion in the Confederate cavalry which held that the best firearm for general use was a double-barreled shotgun. That these came into use at all was simply due to an appeal, early in the war, for public-spirited Confederate citizens to donate guns for the Army's use, and most of the weapons so donated were sporting shotguns. They were all muzzle-loaders, and after some time in service generally had their barrels cut back to about 20 inches' length. Bedford Forrest's cavalry carried their 12-gauge guns in saddle scabbards, and habitually kept them loaded with 12 buckshot to each barrel. This, discharged into infantry or artillery during a spirited charge, was a fearsome weapon. But as more formal weapons, particularly carbines, began to appear in some numbers the shotgun declined in popularity, largely because the sporting shotgun is a less robust weapon than a service rifle or carbine. However, shotguns never entirely disappeared from service, though in the latter part of the war their use seems to have been largely by irregular and guerrilla forces.

Pistols

There was no official model of pistol with either the Union or the Confederate Armies, and the Union Army did not undertake pistol manufacture, preferring to leave that in the hands of private companies and simply contract for what was wanted. There were two standard calibers, the 'Army' of .44 and the 'Navy' of .36, though this was, in fact, a Colt commercial designation

Below: The Savage .36 Navy model revolver with a rare fitted shoulder stock and long-range sight.

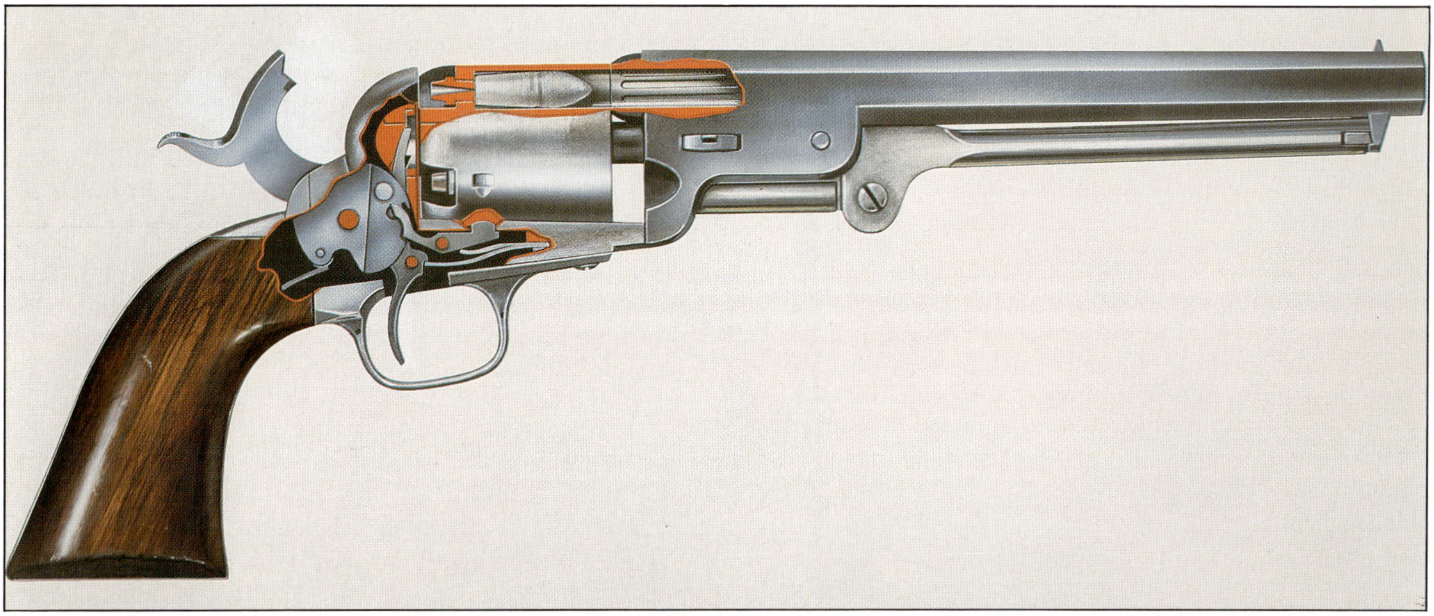

Above: A sectioned view of the Colt .36 Navy revolver Model 1851.

Below: The Colt .36 Navy revolver, showing the operation of the rammer in reloading from the front of the chamber.

and many soldiers preferred the .36 caliber as being a more handy weapon.

Undoubtedly the Colt revolver was the most common, and there were three principal models which made up the bulk of the Colt pistols used in the Civil War.

The first of these was the Model 1851 Navy revolver, which appeared in 1850 and was to remain in production until 1873, some 215,000 being made. The 1851 Navy was in .36 caliber, had a six-shot cylinder, a 7.5-inch octagonal barrel with attached loading lever, case-hardened frame, hammer and rammer lever with the remaining metal blued, and one-piece walnut grips. The grip straps were of silver-plated brass, though a few in blued steel were also made. The cylinder was roll-engraved on its outer surface with a scene showing a battle between the Texas Navy and that of Mexico.

There are a number of variant models of the 1851, since minor details of manufacture were changed from time to time, and some will be found with the butt slotted to take a detachable stock, turning the pistol into a passable carbine.

The second important model is the Navy of 1861. This remained in production from 1861 until 1873, some 38,800 being made. In general it is to the same specification as the earlier model, a .36 caliber six-shot with a 7.5-inch barrel, but the barrel is rounded and has a somewhat different style of rammer. One of the most notable features is the 'streamlined' way in which the barrel is

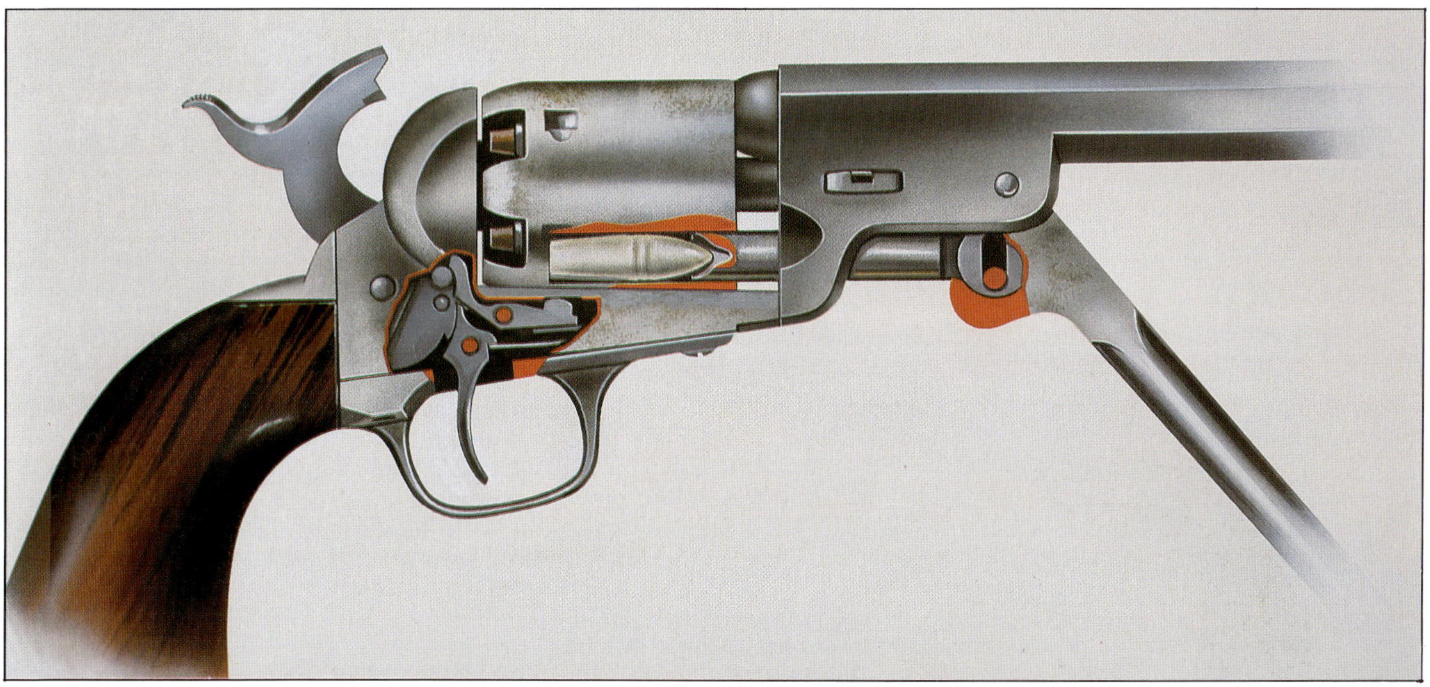

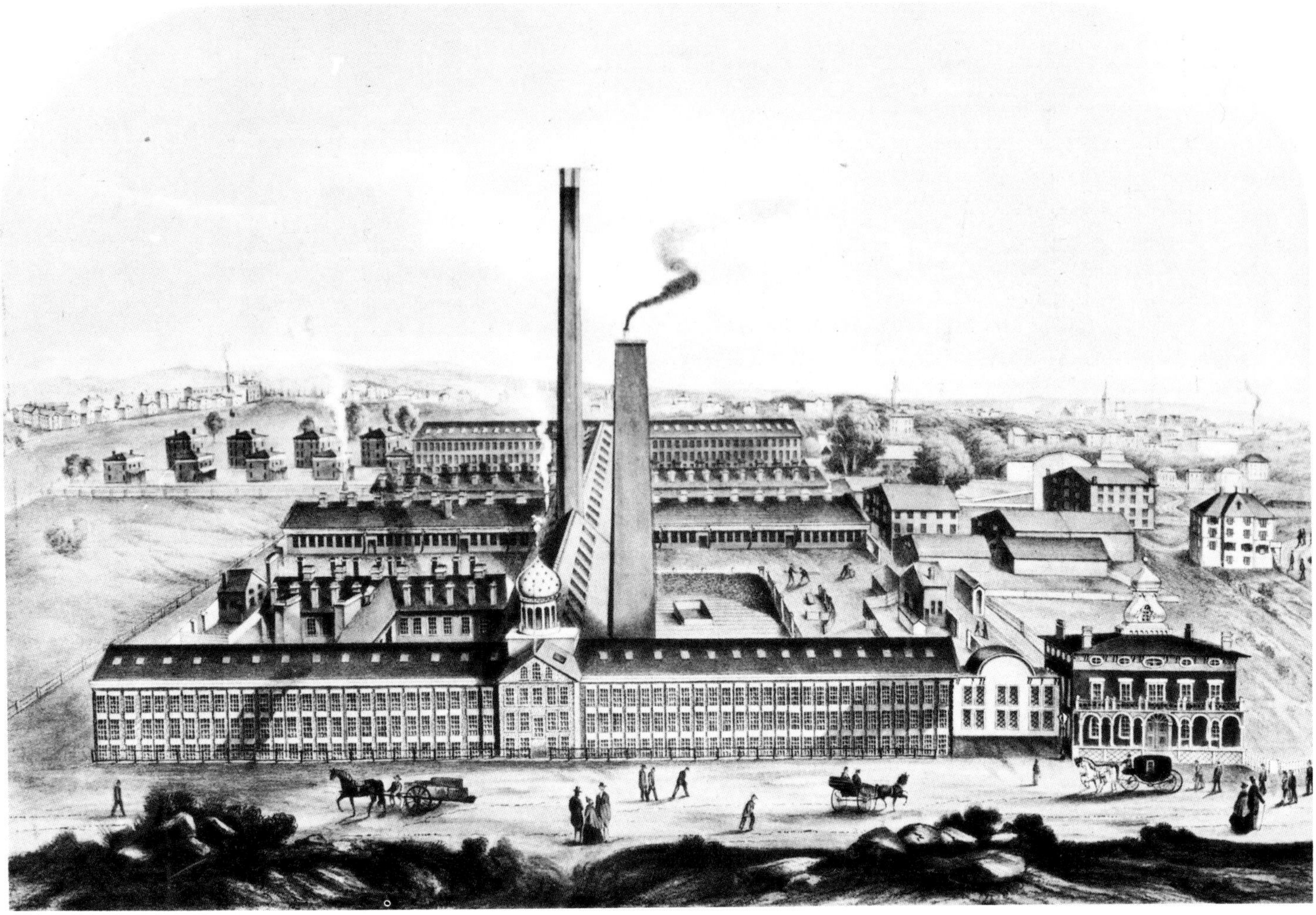

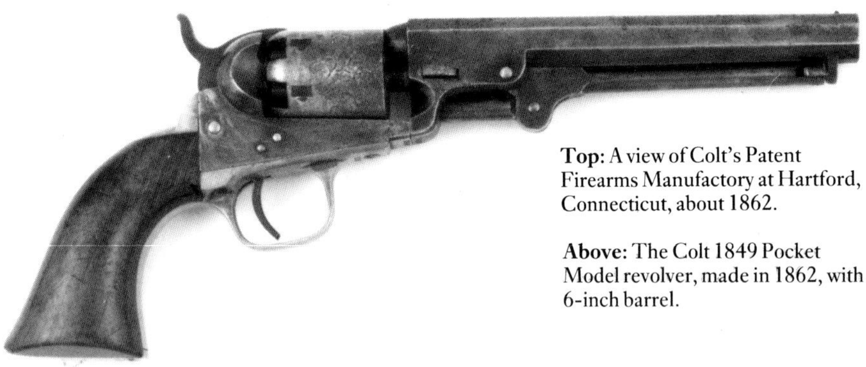

Top: A view of Colt's Patent Firearms Manufactory at Hartford, Connecticut, about 1862.

Above: The Colt 1849 Pocket Model revolver, made in 1862, with 6-inch barrel.

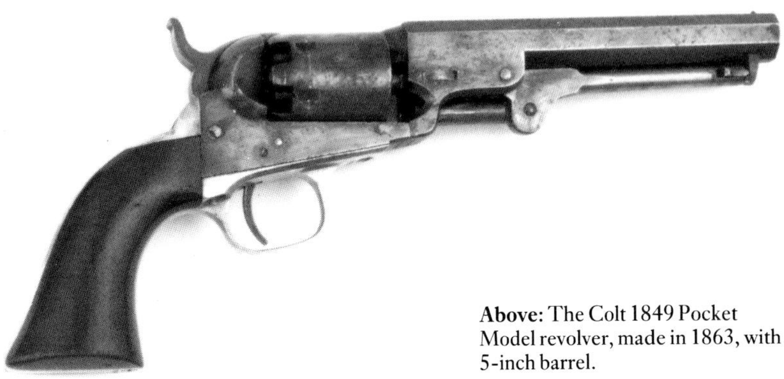

Above: The Colt 1849 Pocket Model revolver, made in 1863, with 5-inch barrel.

blended into the chambered area, and the general smoothness of the weapon. Most will be found with the same Texas-Mexico navy battle scene engraved on the cylinder, though a very small number were made with fluted and unengraved cylinders. An equally limited number of shoulder-stock models was produced. A total of 17,010 of both models of Navy revolver was bought by the Union authorities for issue, but since the pistol was in commercial manufacture well before the war and throughout the war, far more than these undoubtedly reached actual service, even if without official blessing.

The third model, of which no less than 129,730 were purchased, was the .44 Army Model of 1860. As with the Navy models, production of this continued until 1873, a total of over 200,000 being made, so again it is reasonable to assume that numbers of privately owned Army models saw combat. The Army Model was a six-shot weapon, with a 'rebated cylinder', meaning that the rear of the cylinder was turned to a smaller diameter than the front. The barrel (7.5 inches in early production, eight inches later) was rounded and smoothed into the frame, as was the Navy Model. The frame, hammer and rammer lever were case-hardened, the remainder blued; grips were of one-piece walnut; and the

Above: Samuel Colt, with one of his products; an engraving from a contemporary photograph.

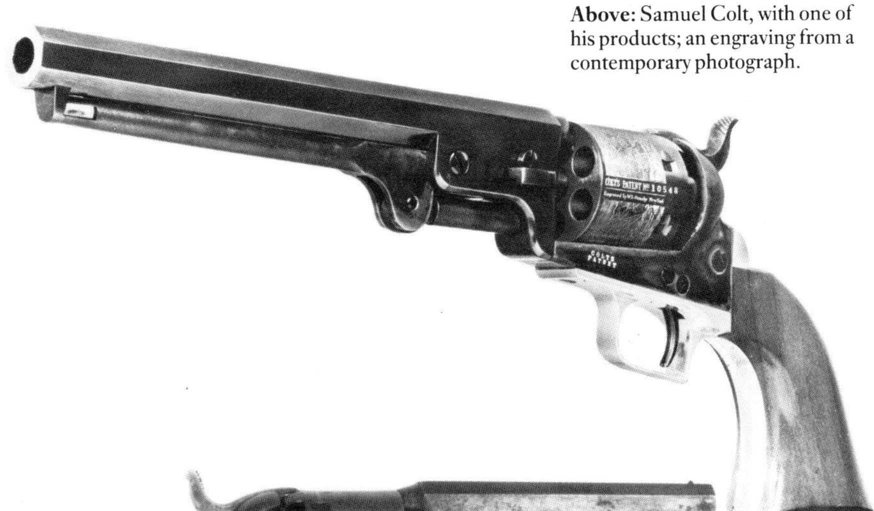

Above: A Colt .36 Navy Model of 1851 with engraved cylinder.

Left: A Colt 1849 Pocket Model revolver, made in 1863, with 4-inch barrel.

trigger-guard and front grip strap were of brass while the backstrap was blued. Strangely, although this was the 'Army' Model, the cylinder was roll-engraved with the same naval battle scene that graced the Navy revolvers!

The .44 Army replaced the 'Third Model Dragoon' in production, and since this latter had been manufactured since 1851 a number of them went to war in the hands of their owners. The Dragoons are powerful and heavy weapons, often jokingly referred to as the 'Colt four-pounder'. The Third Model is identified by a rounded barrel forged in a slab-sided frame giving it a part-round, part-octagonal appearance. The six-shot cylinder is engraved with a scene depicting a fight between Texas Rangers and Indians. Some models were fitted for shoulder stocks. There is also the relatively rare 'Hartford English Dragoon' model; the parts for these were made in Hartford but assembly was done in London for sale in Britain, and as a result the weapons are marked with English London proof marks. There are innumerable minor variations to be found in this particular model, since Colt supplied his London factory with all the rag-tag of stock components left over from earlier Dragoon models, so that minor details such as the trigger-guard and mainsprings differ. Some 200 of these pistols were sent back from London to Hartford in 1861 and were sold for use in the war.

The Model 1849 Pocket Revolver was made from 1849 to 1873; it was the most common of all Colt percussion revolvers, some 325,000 being made, and several hundreds, if not thousands, must have been privately taken to the war. The Pocket Model was in .31 caliber, with five- or six-shot cylinders, octagonal barrels of three-, four-, five- or six-inch length, with or without attached loading levers. The cylinder was roll-engraved with a scene depicting a stagecoach hold-up.

The next most important issue revolver after the Colt was that of Eli Remington. Like the Colt, this came in 'Army' .44 caliber and 'Navy' .36 caliber versions. The Army Model 1861 differed from Colt's design in one significant respect, that it had a solid frame. In other words the frame of the pistol extended from the barrel, across the top of the cylinder, to meet the standing breech. It was forged as one unit, slotted for the cylinder, and was thus a far stronger weapon than the Colt. Another recognition point is the 'web' of steel beneath the barrel, extending down to the front of the frame. The cylinder had six chambers, the barrel was eight inches long and octagonal, and the entire gun was blued except for the hammer which was case-hardened. The total number of Model 1861 made is in some doubt, but is believed not to exceed 12,000. Almost every one was taken by the Union Army, and specimens without military markings are uncommon.

The Model 1861 Navy was practically the same design as the Army, but smaller, as befitted

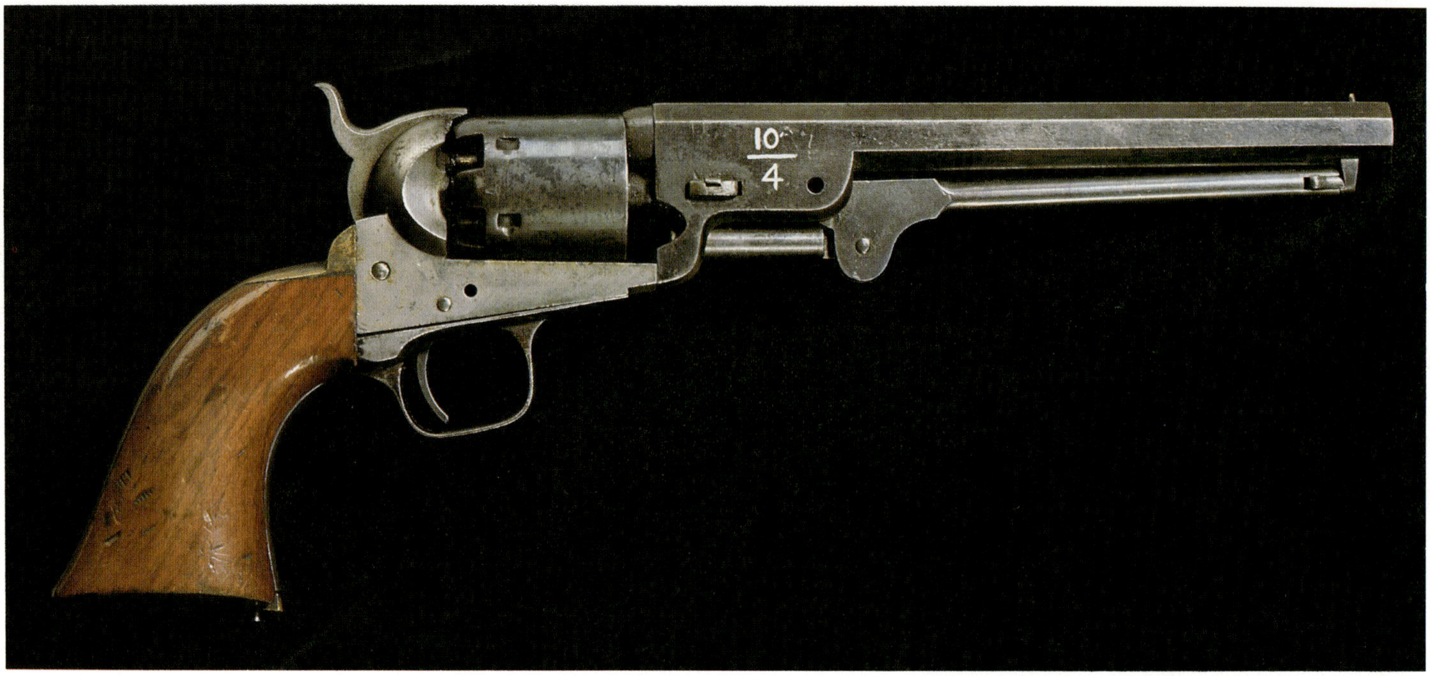

Above: Another view of a .36 Navy Colt revolver, with plain blued finish.

Below: The Remington .44 caliber 'Old Army' Model revolver of 1861.

Far right: Captain Schwarz, of the Union Army, displaying his prowess with a .36 Savage & North 'Figure 8' revolver.

its .36 caliber. The barrel was 7.375 inches long and, as with the Army Model, almost the entire production of perhaps 8500 was taken by the Union Army and unmarked models are rare.

In 1863 the Model 1861 Army was replaced by the 'New Model Army'. This differed only in detail from the 1861 Army, being generally strengthened and improved so as to make manufacture easier. Altogether 125,314 Remington Army revolvers were purchased by the Union, and over 110,000 of these must have been the New Model.

In a similar manner, 1863 also saw the 'New Navy' Model appear. Again, this was little more than an improved version of the 'Old Navy' of 1861. Of these 1901 were bought by the Union Army, and a further 4344 by the Union Navy.

The Colt and Remington were fairly conventional weapons; the same cannot be said for the next Union arm, the Savage Navy Model. This stemmed from a design known as the 'Savage & North Figure of Eight' revolver which first appeared in 1856 and got its odd descriptive name from the shape of the double trigger. In fact this consisted of a ring trigger beneath a conventional trigger, though the shape often makes this hard to appreciate. The Savage & North had a six-shot .36 caliber cylinder; on pulling back the ring trigger, this cylinder was thrust forward so that the mouth of the aligned chamber enclosed the rear end of the barrel, and at the same time the hammer was cocked. The firer could now take aim and pull the upper trigger which released the hammer to fire the shot. Pushing the ring trigger back released the cylinder and revolved it, ready for the next shot.

The Figure of Eight revolver appeared in four different models between 1856 and 1859, and it

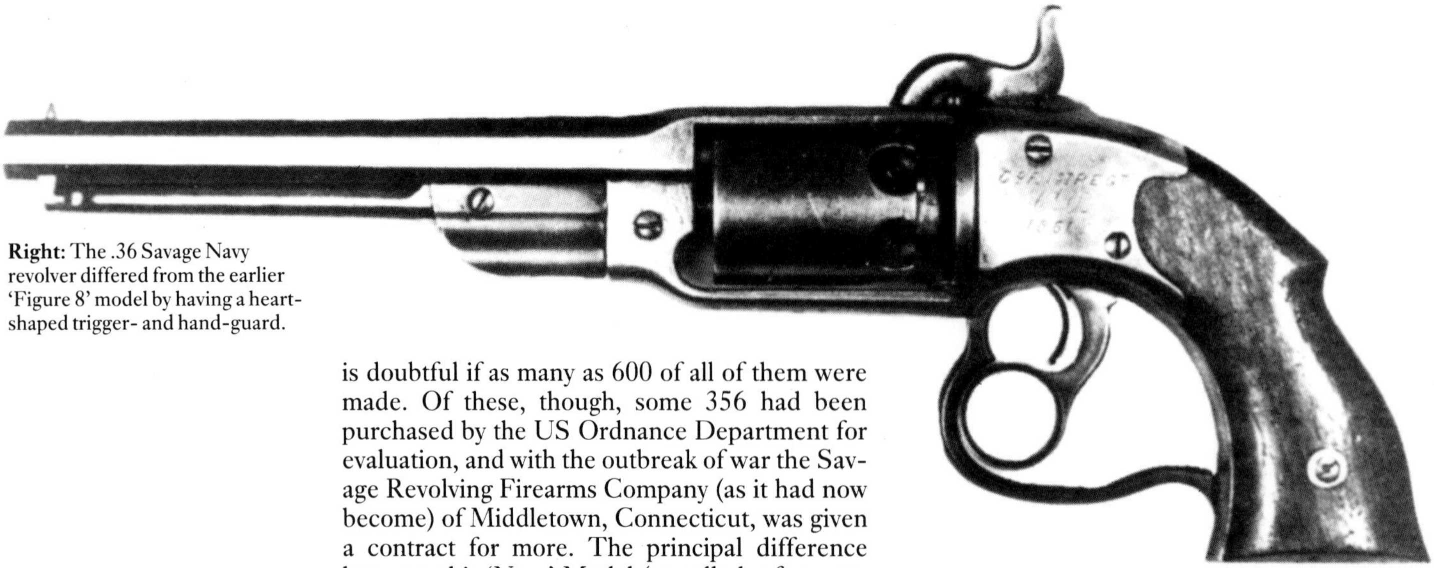

Right: The .36 Savage Navy revolver differed from the earlier 'Figure 8' model by having a heart-shaped trigger- and hand-guard.

is doubtful if as many as 600 of all of them were made. Of these, though, some 356 had been purchased by the US Ordnance Department for evaluation, and with the outbreak of war the Savage Revolving Firearms Company (as it had now become) of Middletown, Connecticut, was given a contract for more. The principal difference between this 'Navy' Model (so called, of course, because it was in .36 caliber) and its forerunners was that the new pattern protected the ring and standard triggers inside a heart-shaped trigger-guard. About 20,000 of these pistols were made by the end of the Civil War, of which 11,284 were purchased by the Union Army, the remainder being sold commercially.

The Starr Arms Company of New York had begun making a unique self-cocking revolver in the middle 1850s. Except for the lockwork, it was a conventional percussion six-shot weapon, in .36 caliber, but although it had a prominent hammer, this could not be cocked by using the thumb for single-action firing. The only way a Starr could be fired was by pulling through on the trigger to lift and drop the hammer. As with other designs, Starr developed two types for sale, an 'Army 1858' in .44 caliber and a 'Navy 1858' in .36 caliber, and numbers of these were bought by the US Army and Navy in pre-war days. On the outbreak of war they bought up the remainder of Starr's stock of these two pistols but persuaded him that he would be more likely to gain a contract if he developed a more conventional type of lock. Starr took the hint and, in 1863, produced his 'Single Action Army' in .44 caliber. This had a six-shot cylinder and eight-inch round barrel with lever rammer underneath, and was a simple single-action model in which the hammer was cocked first and released by the trigger. This met

Below: A Starr .44 caliber double-action Army revolver, Model of 1858.

with official approval and 17,952 were purchased. Starr also made them for the civil market, and doubtless several thousand of these went to war as well.

One of the most prized revolvers, by those who managed to obtain one, was the Whitney Navy Model. Made by Eli Whitney Jr, this was a .36 caliber solid-frame six-shot weapon with a standard barrel length of 7.5 inches (though other lengths are known). The barrel was octagonal, with a lever rammer beneath, and the lock was single-action. There are several minor variations of design. The First Model, which appeared in about 1859, is generally marked 'Eagle Co', though nobody has ever found a good reason for this. The Second Model, most of which went to the Union Army, used a heavier frame and a brass trigger-guard. However, within these models there were further changes, such as the number of rifling grooves and the shape and size of the trigger-guard. Altogether 7602 Whitney revolvers were bought by the Union Army and 5726 by the Union Navy, with a further 792 purchased by the New Jersey State Militia.

The Rogers & Spencer Company of Willowvale, New York, were subcontractors to C S Pettengill of New Haven, and manufactured Pettengill's 'Army Model' revolver for the Union Army in the early 1860s. The Pettengill is an odd-looking weapon, since the butt rises to straight behind the cylinder, giving it a strangely hunched appearance. The revolver was, of course, in .44 caliber, with a six-shot cylinder and an octagonal 7½-inch barrel with rammer lever beneath. There was no visible hammer, and the lock was self-cocking, requiring the trigger to be pulled through for each shot. About 2000 of these were bought by the Union, but their ordnance inspectors constantly found defects and insisted on several minor modifications, with the result that there are several variant models of Pettengill to be found. Rogers & Spencer, doubtless upset by this, decided to abandon the Pettengill design and develop something of their own which would be more conventional and more reliable, and they designed a straightforward .44 single-action pistol. Unfortunately, although their revolver was accepted for service, and they received a contract for 5000, by the time they got into production the war was over. The pistols were delivered, but were never used and in 1901 were sold off, unfired, as surplus stock.

Below: Two Wesson and Leavitt revolvers made by the Massachusetts Arms Co. The upper is the 'Belt Model', the lower, dismantled to show the mechanism, is the 'Dragoon Model'. Though manufactured in 1850-51, many found use in the war.

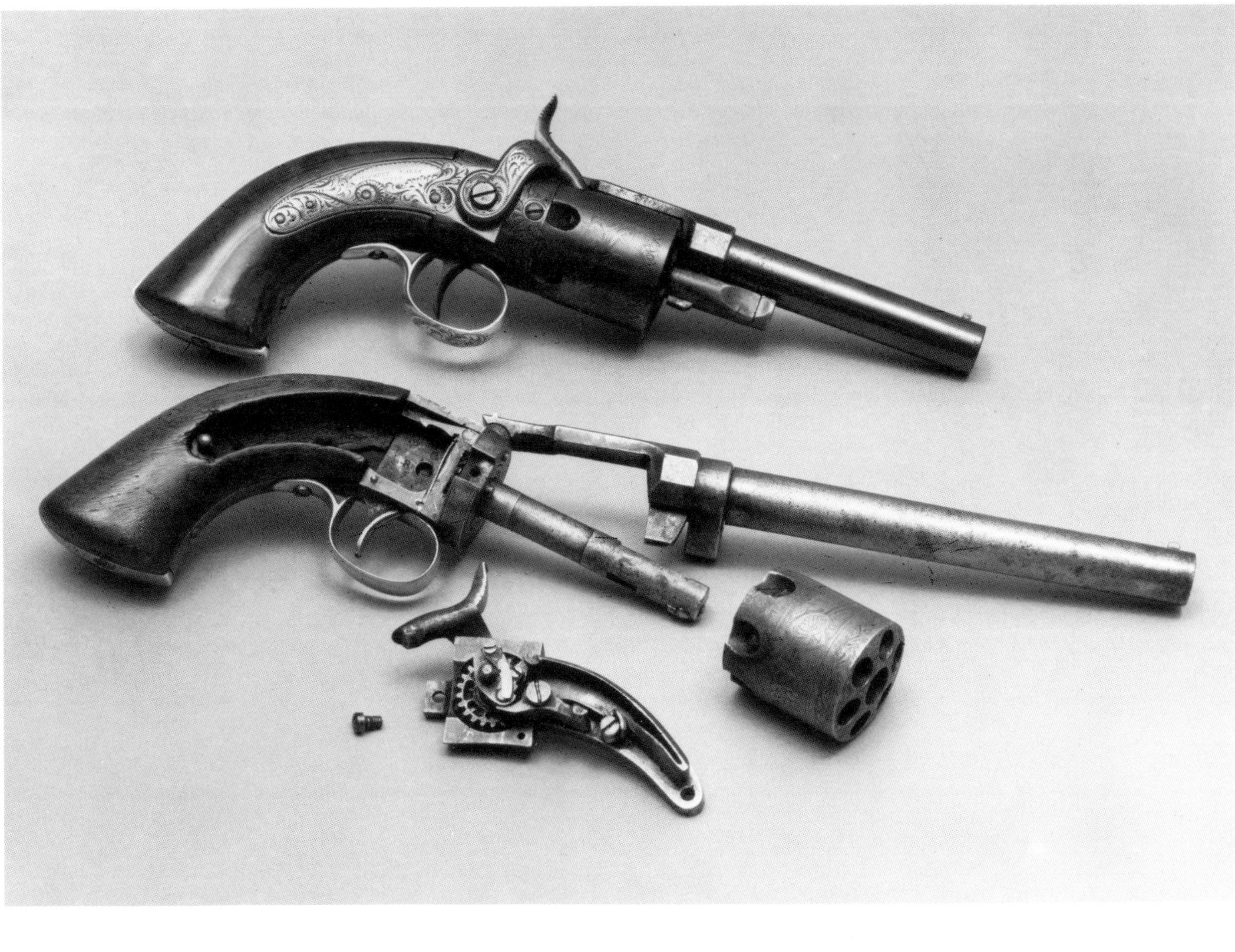

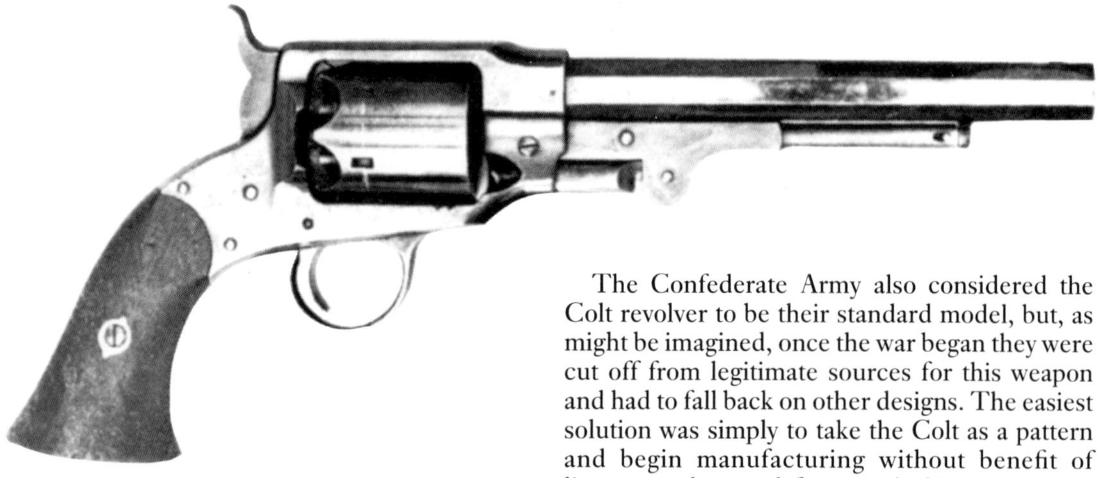

Right: The .44 Rogers & Spencer revolver, few of which were delivered before the war ended.

A pistol frequently thought to be Confederate is the Shawk & Maclanahan Navy revolver, manufactured in St Louis, Missouri, in 1858. In fact Shawk and Maclanahan were Union sympathizers, but since the pistols were sold on the commercial market some of them inevitably found their way to the Confederate side and have been assumed to be of Confederate manufacture. The S&M was a single-action .36 caliber six-shot weapon with an eight-inch round barrel and a long rammer lever beneath. It was an elegant weapon, but only about a hundred were made and they are extremely rare.

In 1853 the English revolver maker Robert Adams visited the USA and appears to have entered into an agreement with the Massachusetts Arms Company of Chicopee Falls whereby they were to have the rights to manufacture the Adams revolver. Due to Colt's patents getting in the way, they were unable to do this until 1858, and they then began making the Beaumont-Adams double-action revolver in .31 and .36 calibers. These were solid-frame five-shot pistols with octagonal barrels and did not carry rammer levers, the cylinders being released by a quick-acting latch for reloading. The 'Navy' Model used a six-inch barrel and of the thousand or so made, 415 were purchased by the Union Army.

The Confederate Army also considered the Colt revolver to be their standard model, but, as might be imagined, once the war began they were cut off from legitimate sources for this weapon and had to fall back on other designs. The easiest solution was simply to take the Colt as a pattern and begin manufacturing without benefit of license, and several firms took this course. For the sake of simplicity we might as well consider them in alphabetical order.

The Augusta Machine Works of Augusta, Georgia, made about a hundred of a copy of the Colt Navy 1851 Model. It had the usual six-shot cylinder, an octagonal barrel with rammer, and was browned all over except for the brass grip straps. The pistol was well made of good material, and the Augusta Machine Works is believed to have been a Confederate government installation built for the purpose, which makes one wonder why only a hundred pistols were turned out in four years.

The Columbus Firearms Manufacturing Company of Columbus, Georgia, also produced a version of the Colt Navy of 1851 in 1863-64. The company was actually given a formal contract by the CSA Army in August 1862 to produce 10,000 Navy revolvers. Production was slow in starting, and after about a hundred had been made, the owners decided early in 1864 they had had enough and sold their factory to the Confederate Government. The Government had plans to turn the factory into the Columbus Arsenal and Armory, but the whole project faltered and eventually the machinery was moved to Macon, Georgia. In 1865, Union troops captured the Columbus plant and destroyed it. It is doubt-

Right: The .36 Colt Model 1862 Police Model revolver, many of which saw service in the hands of individuals who purchased them privately.

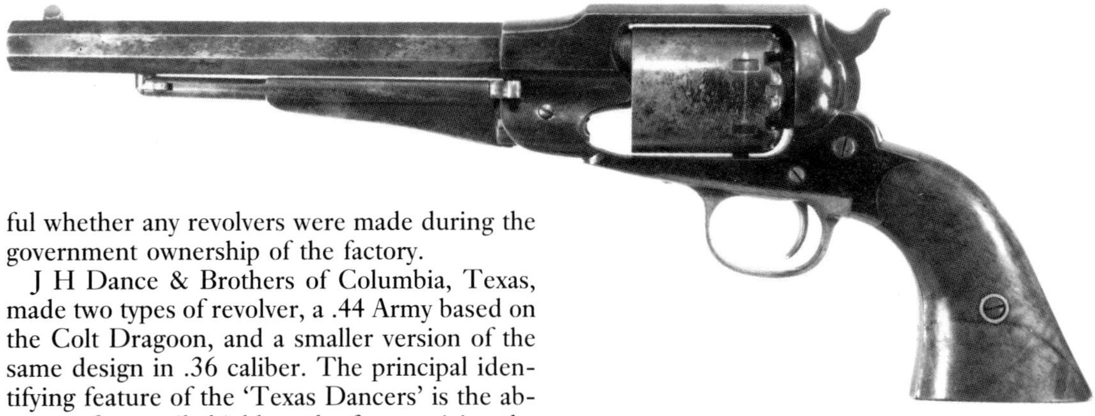

Right: The Remington .44 'New Army' Model of 1863.

ful whether any revolvers were made during the government ownership of the factory.

J H Dance & Brothers of Columbia, Texas, made two types of revolver, a .44 Army based on the Colt Dragoon, and a smaller version of the same design in .36 caliber. The principal identifying feature of the 'Texas Dancers' is the absence of a recoil shield on the frame, giving the revolver a peculiar slab-sided appearance. About 350 of .44 caliber and 150 in .36 caliber were made between 1862 and 1863. The Government of Texas thought sufficiently highly of their product to exempt the workforce from military service. In 1863 the company decided to move their factory from Columbia since it was thought to be vulnerable to gunfire from Union gunboats sailing up the river, and they resettled in a new location a few miles away. This stopped the production of revolvers, which was never resumed.

Griswold and Gunnison of Griswoldville, Georgia, were probably the most prolific Confederate Colt copyists. From 1862 to 1864 they turned out about 3700 .36 caliber Navy models based on the Colt 1851. Due to a shortage of iron these had a brass frame, with a Dragoon-type iron barrel 7.5 inches long. Griswold was, in fact, a displaced Northerner who sympathized with the South and set up in business making pikes for the CSA. From this he went on to making the revolvers against an official CSA contract. The factory was captured by Union troops in 1864.

The Leech and Rigdon revolver was another near-Colt, first made in Columbus, Mississippi, and then in Greensboro, Georgia. In .36 caliber, this was a six-shot model with a 7.5-inch Dragoon-type barrel and loading lever. The two men, Leech and Rigdon, first set up in business in Memphis, Tennessee, as the Memphis Novelty Works, and when the war broke out they concentrated on swordmaking. They then moved to Columbus and began making revolvers, the first production being marked 'Leech & Rigdon Novelty Works'. Early in 1863 they moved to Greensboro and received a contract from the CSA for the entire output of their factory. But in January 1864 they agreed to disagree and separated. Leech set up his own workshop as Leech & Co and continued to produce revolvers, making perhaps a hundred. Rigdon moved to Augusta, Georgia, and set up as Rigdon, Ansley & Co, assuming the responsibility for the balance of the CSA contract. Here he produced about five hundred revolvers to complete the contract, and then went on to make about a thousand more; these differed from the original model by having twelve cylinder stops instead of the usual six. It is believed that something in the order of three thousand revolvers were made in the various shifts and changes of this company, plus the thousand or so Rigdon and Ansley type. Manufacture was halted by Sherman's occupation of Georgia in 1865.

The Schneider & Glassick revolver was made in Memphis, Tennessee in 1861-62, and probably no more than fifty were produced. It was the usual copy of the 1851 Colt Navy and was apparently of good quality, being produced by

Right: A London-made Adams Model 1857 revolver; many were imported and employed by both armies.

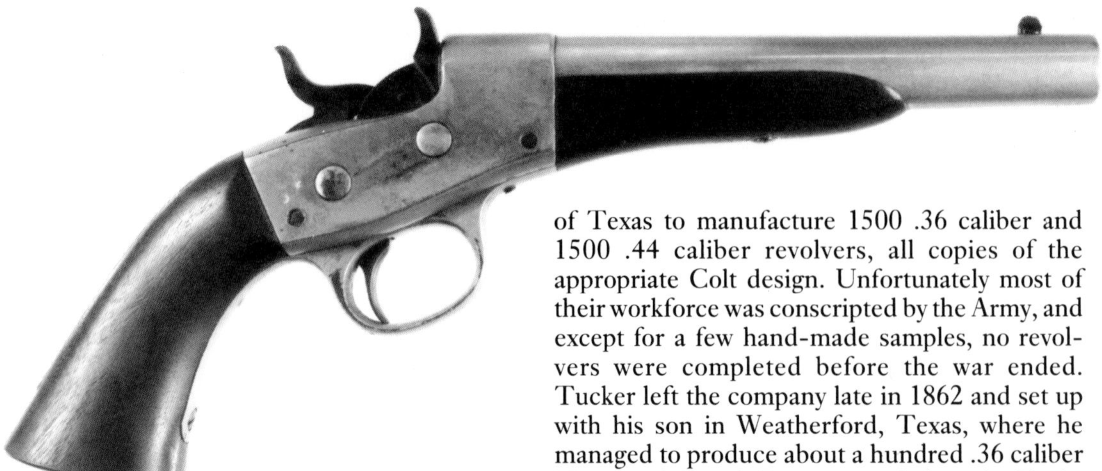

Right: The Remington .50 caliber Navy single-shot rolling block pistol. This is the 1867 model, very slightly different from the 1865, a few of which were issued before the war ended.

two men who were properly trained gunsmiths. They also appear to have made a slightly different version with a Dragoon-style barrel, though there is a theory which suggests that this was actually made by someone else and stamped with Schneider & Glassick's name. Since only three specimens (two 1851s, one Dragoon-style) are known to exist, the Schneider & Glassick has to remain something of a mystery.

George Todd of Austin, Texas, was another trained gunsmith and he manufactured his own version of the Colt shortly before the war broke out. Specimens are known with part-round, part-octagonal barrels and with full octagonal barrels. In .36 caliber, these are rare weapons and their association with the CSA can only be assumed, since at the outbreak of war Todd stopped manufacturing and went back to his native state of Alabama to take up work in a government arsenal.

In April 1862 Tucker, Sherrard & Co of Lancaster, Texas, accepted a contract from the State of Texas to manufacture 1500 .36 caliber and 1500 .44 caliber revolvers, all copies of the appropriate Colt design. Unfortunately most of their workforce was conscripted by the Army, and except for a few hand-made samples, no revolvers were completed before the war ended. Tucker left the company late in 1862 and set up with his son in Weatherford, Texas, where he managed to produce about a hundred .36 caliber Navy models with Dragoon-style barrels. Tucker, Sherrard now became Taylor, Sherrard, but although the company managed to produce stocks of parts, no assembly of revolvers took place until well after the war.

Turning now to more original designs, we can begin with the Cofer revolver, which was made by T W Cofer of Portsmouth, Virginia. Cofer held a CSA patent (No. 9) which covered an unusual split cylinder capable of being loaded with a prepared metallic cartridge which was simply an auxiliary chamber with a percussion nipple on the end. The revolvers made to this patent were in .36 caliber and were solid-framed, based on the Whitney design. Very few were made, however, before Cofer saw the light and began making the revolver with a conventional cylinder. The only aberrant feature of these revolvers is the presence of a sheathed trigger rather than the usual trigger and guard.

Another design based on the solid-frame Whitney was that of Spiller and Burr of Atlanta. This was a brass-framed .36 caliber model with octagonal barrel. The company received a CSA contract for no less than 15,000 revolvers in 1862, when they were located in Richmond, Virginia. They moved to Atlanta and began production, where they made something between 750 and

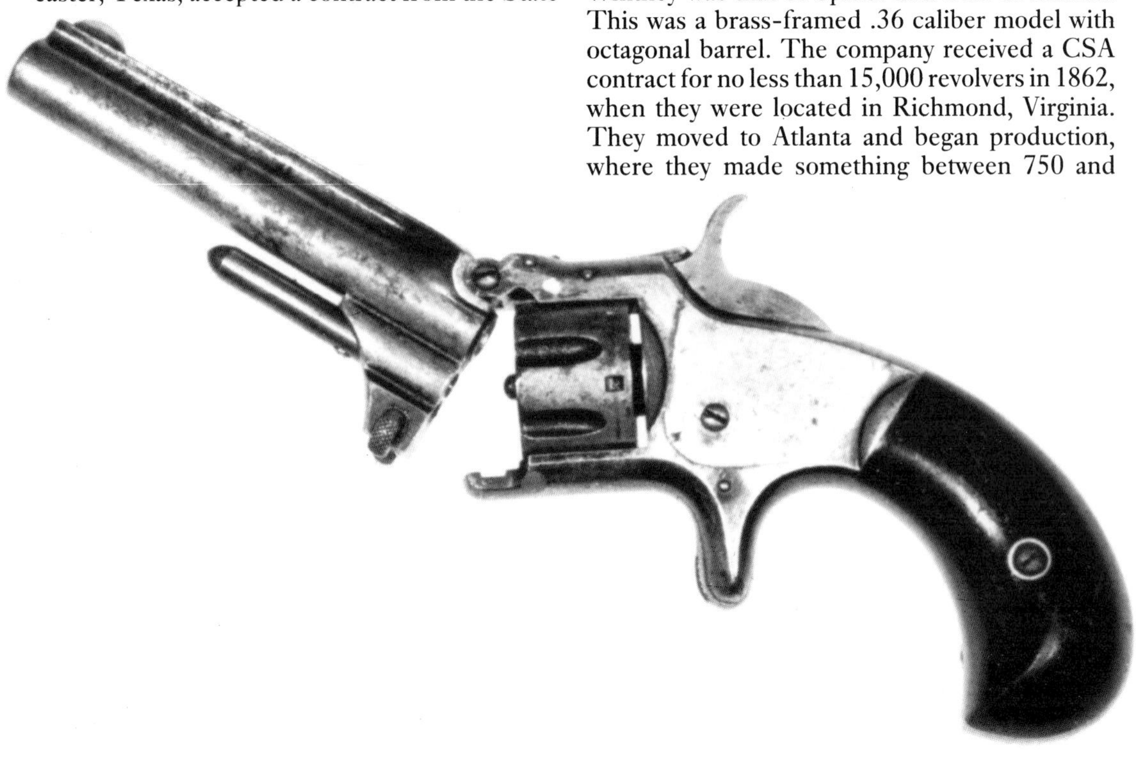

Right: The Smith & Wesson 'First Model, Second Issue' .22 caliber revolver, showing the 'tip-up' method of reloading by removal of the cylinder.

Right: The Leech & Rigdon .36 revolver, a copy of the Colt Model 1851.

800 revolvers. In January 1864 the CSA government bought the factory and moved the plant to Macon, Georgia, where they were able to make another 700 or so before Sherman's approach in November 1864 terminated manufacture.

The last of the Confederate revolvers is the LeMat, a most remarkable weapon, and one with a rather tangled history. Dr Alexandre Le Mat was a medical man in New Orleans when he appears to have been inspired to invent a revolver, and in 1856 he took out a patent for using a second barrel as the axis for a revolver cylinder. In 1859 he improved on his idea by patenting a hammer which would allow the position of the firing pin to be selected so that it would fire either the chambers of the cylinder or the axial barrel. The point of the whole design was that the cylinder, and its associated conventional barrel, would be used for bullets in the normal way, but the barrel forming the axis of the cylinder would be charged with lead shot, so that the firer could have a formidable last-ditch defense available.

A prototype was manufactured in Philadelphia, by a gunsmith called John Krider, in 1859 and Le Mat set up a small factory in New Orleans where about three hundred are believed to have been made. Le Mat was aided in this enterprise by P T Beauregard who, when the Civil War broke out, became one of the Confederates' better generals. Possibly as a result of this connection, Le Mat received a contract to provide revolvers to the CSA, but for various reasons he decided to have them manufactured in France and shipped back to the Confederacy. It appears that the quality of manufacture was poor, and Le Mat moved his base of operations to Britain where the French revolvers were reworked into operating condition and the remainder of the revolvers were made. Precisely who made them is not known; the guns are marked 'Le Mat & Girard's Patent London' but will be found to carry Birmingham proofmarks, which suggests that they were made in that city, possibly by the Birmingham Small Arms Company. Serial numbers of Le Mat revolvers go as high as 9000, but they appear to have been applied erratically and it is doubtful if more than about 1500 were delivered. Le Mat continued to make revolvers, and some revolving carbines, after the Civil War.

The 'standard' Le Mat is of .42 caliber and has a nine-shot cylinder allied to a 6.5-inch barrel. The axis on which the cylinder revolves is a .63 caliber five-inch smoothbore barrel which accepted a load of buckshot. Firing was by the usual form of percussion cap fitted to nipples behind each chamber and to a special nipple on the frame for the shot barrel. The firing pin could be switched to align with either the cylinder nipples or the frame nipple as required. There was also a 'Baby' Le Mat in .32 caliber, also with a nine-shot cylinder and with a 4.25-inch octagonal barrel. The shot barrel in this model was .41 caliber and 2.75 inches long. The CSA ordered 2000 of these revolvers but it is believed that no more than one hundred were ever made.

Right: A Le Mat Grapeshot revolver, Second Model, with a 9-shot .42 caliber cylinder and a .63 caliber buckshot barrel.

2
THE INFANTRY AND ITS WEAPONS

Previous page: A Union 'Sharpshooter' using a rifle with telescopic sight.

Infantry formed the bulk of both armies during the Civil War – 'as it was in the beginning, is now, and ever shall be' it was the foot soldier who took the brunt of the combat. The Union Army eventually raised no less than 1666 infantry regiments, plus a further 306 independent infantry companies. According to the regulations of 1861 a volunteer infantry regiment would consist of ten companies each led by a captain and having two lieutenants, 13 NCOs, 2 buglers, a wagoner and a maximum of 82 private soldiers. In addition there was a regimental headquarters amounting to six officers, a chaplain, two NCOs, a hospital orderly and 26 bandsmen. Thus a volunteer regiment at full establishment had a total strength of 1046 officers and men. The regular infantry regiment differed in its organization, being split into two battalions each with eight companies, so that its full strength was close to 1700 of all ranks. However, it is doubtful if this figure of regiments raised actually represents anything like the figure of actual men available for duty at any give time, and since it is generally accepted that the Union raised a total of 1.5 million men during the course of the war it seems reasonable to assume that, allowing for the requirements of the other arms and services, the Union infantry strength was probably fairly static at about half a million men. Which makes it all the more remarkable that the total Union purchases of infantry rifles and muskets during the war amounted to 1,565,250 weapons of over thirty different types.

The Confederate infantry regiment was of similar size and organization to the Union volunteer regiment, with just over 1000 officers and men when at full strength. Full strength was rarely attained, and the more general figure was in the region of 750 all ranks.

The Confederate Army mustered a total of about one million men – which, from an eligible population of only 1.14 million, was a remarkable feat. Assuming about half these to have been infantry, and assuming the loss and replacement rate to be the same, it seems reasonable to suppose that the Confederates purchased something like the same one and a half million rifles. Unfortunately, while there are fairly good records of the contracts issued by the Confederate Government and states, the actual number of weapons delivered against such contracts is far from certain, and no reliable figure can be put.

Rifles

The standard infantry weapon, on both sides, was the rifle musket, a piece of terminology which came from Britain and originated with the Duke of Wellington. When rifled longarms were first suggested for the British Army in the 1840s, the Duke agreed that such weapons were necessary but he balked at calling them rifles 'lest the whole army clamour to be clothed in green', the special color appropriate to rifle regiments. So the

Right: Company K, 4th Georgia Volunteers, CSA, parade in 1861.

Enfield weapon became the 'rifle musket' and the term stuck for many years.

The name was correct enough. The weapon was literally the old-time muzzle-loading musket, but fired by percussion and rifled; indeed, early in the war, to meet the sudden demand, many smoothbore flintlock muskets were brought out of store and converted to rifled percussion pattern relatively easily. But the nominal standard US rifle at the outbreak of war was the Model 1855 Percussion Rifle, manufactured at Harper's Ferry Arsenal between 1857 and 1861. This was a .58 caliber rifled muzzle-loader with an external hammer and the Maynard tape primer system of firing. The three-inch barrel was stocked to within the last few inches of the muzzle, sufficient room being left for the ramrod, carried beneath the barrel, to protrude so that it could be easily grasped. The barrel was secured to the stock by two bands which were brass on early models, iron on most production. The stock was of walnut, and there was a patch box let into the right side of the butt. The lock was marked with an eagle motif on the cover of the box into which the Maynard tape was loaded, and US HARPER'S FERRY on the forward part of the lock plate. Although over 7000 of these weapons were made, they are relatively scarce today because of wastage during the war and also because of the number destroyed by fire during the Confederate raid on the Armory in April 1861.

It was immediately obvious that the relatively limited number of M1855 rifles was not going to go very far in outfitting the expanding Union Army, and in 1861 Springfield Armory began manufacture of the Model 1861 US Percussion Rifle Musket. Manufacture of this continued into 1863, over a quarter of a million being made in the Armory and over 450,000 by outside contractors. The Model 1861 was a .58 caliber rifled percussion musket, using a simple hammer and nipple firing mechanism. The barrel was 40 inches long and secured to the stock by three iron barrel bands. The lock plate was marked with the eagle and US SPRINGFIELD, with the date at the rear end of the plate, if made in the Arsenal, with US and the maker's location, sometimes name, and date on contract manufacture.

A variation on this design was the model known as the 'Special Model 1861', entirely made under contract. It appears that this contract was first given to the Colt company, and they produced their own design which, while adhering to the general specification of the Model 1861, differed in details so that parts were not interchangeable with the Armory model. Colt began manufacture in 1861 and continued throughout the war, turning out about 100,000 of which many went to satisfy contracts from individual states. In 1862 manufacture was extended to other companies, who turned out about 80,000 between them.

While the 1861 was in production, the specialists at Springfield Armory looked closely at the design and decided that it would be possible to step up the rate of production by changing some of the details. Instead of browning the barrel, a process which was rather slow, barrels were left bright or, in rare cases, blued; other components

Below: The accidental explosion of a box of 3000 small arms cartridges in a tent of the 3rd New York Volunteers, the type of accident which happened frequently with undisciplined troops.

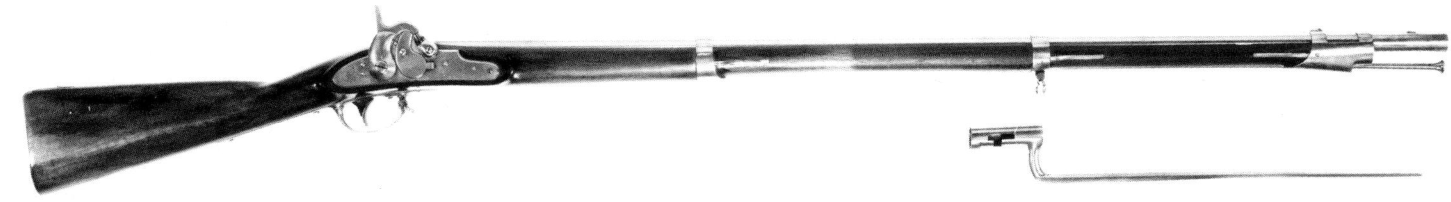

Above: The Springfield Rifle Musket Model of 1855, with socket bayonet and Maynard Tape Primer lock.

were blued or case-hardened. The contour of the hammer was changed to make it easier to manufacture, and the barrel bands were made without the rather complicated retaining springs used in earlier designs. The result went into production in 1863 as the Model 1863 Rifle Musket, and Springfield turned out over 270,000. No outside contracts were let for this weapon, the private manufacturers being left alone to carry on turning out Model 1861s as hard as they could go, though it appears that some of the manufacturing short cuts introduced on the M1863 were adopted by some contractors on their late Model 1861 rifles.

Not satisfied, Springfield again made some simplifications, and the result is generally known as the 'Model 1863 Type 2'. The changes included a single-leaf rear sight instead of the original double-leaf type; solid barrel bands retained by springs set into the stock; a new type of ramrod; and the omission of blue or brown finish on most parts, they being left bright. Production of the Type 2 began in 1864 and over 255,000 were made before the war ended.

In order to satisfy demand during the early part of the war, several thousand Model 1842 percussion muskets were brought out of store and issued. These were the first regulation percussion musket produced for the US Army, having been made at Springfield and Harper's Ferry between 1844 and 1855. They were of .69 caliber with 42-inch barrels secured by three bands, and the side lock carried an external hammer working to a cap nipple. Apart from the percussion lock the Model 1842 was practically the same as its predecessor, the Model 1840 flintlock.

The abandonment of browning or blueing accorded well with the tendency towards 'spit and polish' of many Union commanders, who insisted on their men burnishing their musket barrels until they shone. Even when not so ordered, many men did this as evidence of their smartness. They regretted it when they went into action; there are many reports of Confederate scouts detecting the movement of Union troops because of the sunlight glinting on polished musket barrels. Even moonlight could reflect, as happened at Fredericksburg when Union troops were detected moving into position at night. At Second Bull Run the glint of barrels was visible through the dust raised by the marching men. It took some sharp lessons before this practice was gradually stamped out.

One last regulation arm appeared during the Civil War, the Model 1863 US Double Musket, manufactured by the J P Lindsay Company of New York. The name might suggest a double-barreled weapon, but in fact it had only one barrel which was loaded with two lots of powder and ball. The first cartridge and ball were rammed down the barrel in the usual manner, a wad was then rammed down on top, and a second charge was then loaded. There were two nipples and two hammers. One nipple had a long fire channel leading to a point in the barrel opposite the forward charge, while the other nipple led directly into the chamber in the usual way and was aligned with the first-loaded, rearmost, charge. The firer cocked the hammer for the first charge and pulled the trigger; the cap flashed down the long channel and ignited the forward charge, expelling the bullet. The wad, rammed on top of the rearmost bullet, prevented the flame igniting the rearmost charge. The firer could then cock the other hammer and fire the remaining charge.

That, at least, was the theory. A single trigger was so linked to the hammers that the forward charge was always fired first; obviously, if anything went wrong with this and the rear charge fired first the results would be quite entertaining for onlookers. A more frequent occurrence, however, was simply that the flame from the first charge flashed past the wad and bullet and ignited the second charge so that both went off together, which generally wrecked the gun, and probably did the firer no good either. The Union Army actually bought 1000 of these weapons, but they were not liked, or trusted very much, by the soldiers and most of them appear to have been damaged by misfiring.

In addition to these 'primary' regulation weapons, there was a wide variety of private designs which were taken into use by the Union Army in order to increase the number of available

Below: The Springfield Rifle Musket, Model of 1861, with bayonet. Note that the lock has reverted to the simple percussion cap type.

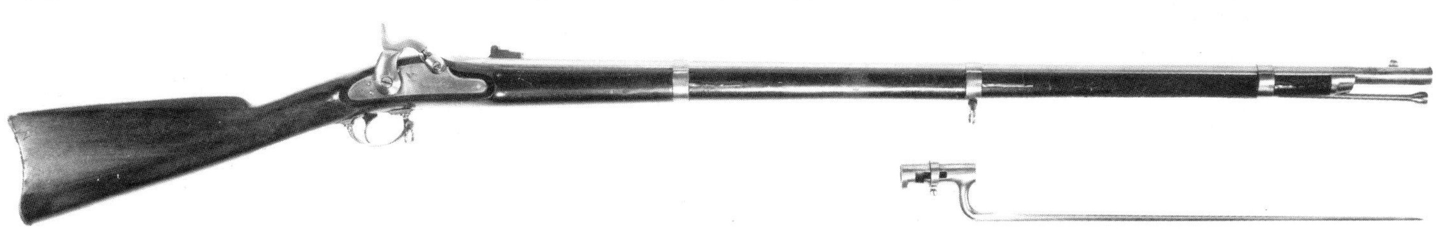

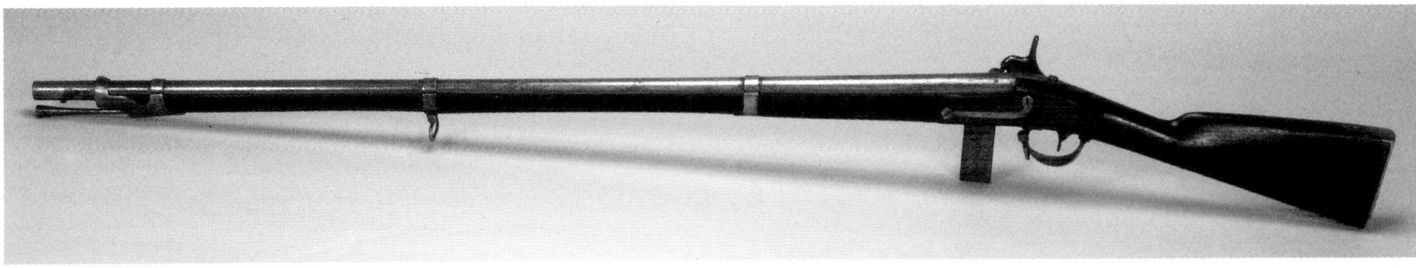

Above: The .69 caliber Model 1840 flintlock musket, converted to Maynard Tape Primer system in about 1848.

weapons, and this applies particularly to breech-loaders. The government arsenals were well set up for turning out muzzle-loaders, and they were content to get on with that; it was largely left to private contractors to develop their ideas about breech loading to a point where the Army could conduct a worthwhile trial, and, if the weapon was thought to be successful, issue a contract.

One of the most unusual of these was the Greene rifle, invented by Lieutenant-Colonel J D Greene of the US Army prior to the war and manufactured from 1859 onwards by the A H Waters Armory of Millbury, Massachusetts. The Greene is remarkable for being one of the earliest bolt action weapons, even though it did not use a metallic cartridge. The bolt was a fairly simple turnbolt which closed the rear end of the barrel but did not contain any sort of firing mechanism. The firer merely opened the bolt by turning it, then removed it and inserted the normal sort of paper cartridge into the chamber, then replaced the bolt. A hammer beneath the gun, in front of the trigger-guard, was then cocked, revealing a nipple. A percussion cap was placed on the nipple, and the trigger pulled so that the hammer flew up and fired the cap.

Although the cartridge was conventional for its day, the bullet was of oval section, and the Greene rifle was oval-bored and the oval twisted, so that the bullet was given the requisite spin. It appears to have been an accurate weapon, and tests showed that the bullet would penetrate seven or eight inches of pine boards at 500 yards range. About four thousand Greene rifles were manufactured, of which 900 were bought by the Union Army and most of the remainder by various state militias.

As well as manufacturing the 'Special M1861 Musket', Colt were, of course, producing pistols as hard as they could, and they also manufactured almost five thousand revolving rifles for the Union Army. Production of these had started in 1856 for the commercial market, but on the outbreak of war the Union authorities immediately contracted to take Colt's output. Two types were made, a five-shot .56 caliber and a six-shot .44 caliber. The design was that of a long rifle (barrel lengths were from 21 to 37.5 inches) with a revolver-type cylinder in the rear, fired by a side-mounted hammer. The cylinder differed from the contemporary Colt revolvers by being fluted, to save weight, and there was a folding rammer lever beneath the stock, attached to the front of the frame.

Opinions differed as to the worth of the Colt revolving rifle. One thousand were issued to Berdan's Sharpshooters in 1862, but there were complaints of all the cylinders firing at once due

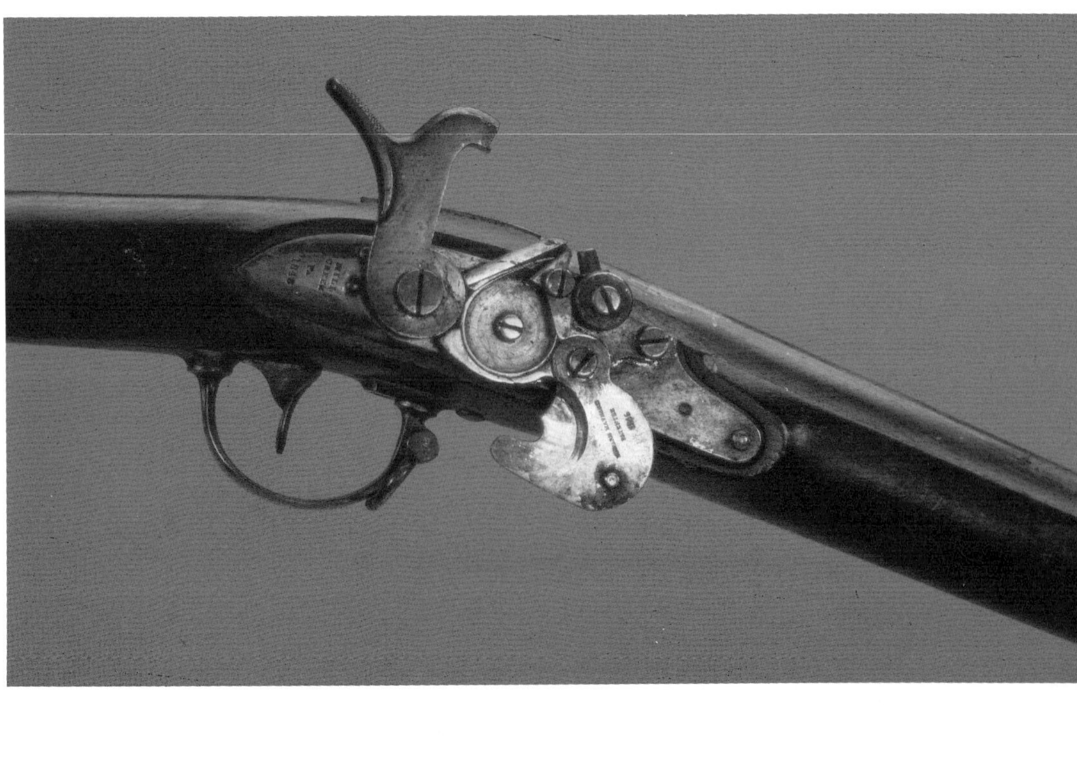

Right: Detail of the Maynard Tape Priming system fitted to the converted 1840 musket. About 2000 such conversions were done in 1848-50.

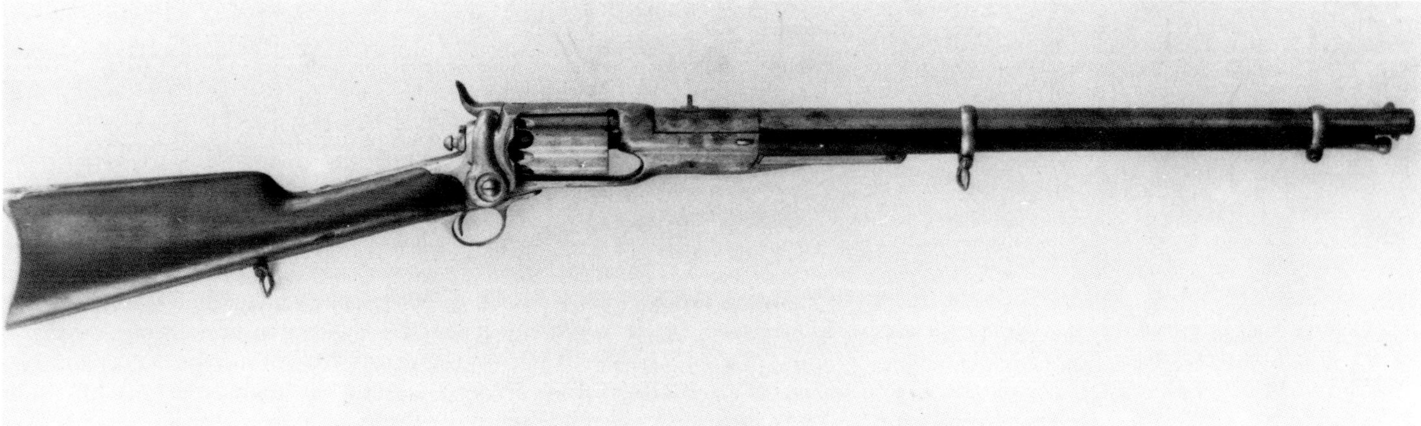

Above: The Colt 1855 Military Model revolving rifle in .56 caliber.

to flash-over, and that even when the guns were working properly the cylinders heated up very quickly, making it dangerous to reload. In May 1862 the Sharpshooters got rid of their Colts and replaced them with Sharps rifles. The proximity of the cylinder to the firer's face made the explosion particularly loud, and there was a constant likelihood of lead shavings, sliced from the bullet when it entered the barrel due to malaligned chambers, spitting back into the firer's face. The worst threat was that if the chambers all fired at once, the firer's forward hand was either amputated or at best severely mangled. The Colt was eventually recommended to be discontinued in service, was withdrawn and sold at scrap prices. It is generally thought doubtful that any official issue of Colt rifles took place after the middle of 1863, though they continued to be sold commercially and many soldiers are believed to have purchased them privately.

The Spencer carbine and its arrival into service is described in the cavalry section; but there was also a Spencer rifle, though it was purchased in much lesser numbers than the carbine, some 11,400 being acquired by the Union Army. The Spencer was a .52 caliber weapon with a 30-inch barrel rifled with six grooves, and it was loaded by inserting a tube holding seven rimfire cartridges into the butt. Operating the under-lever opened the breech and fed one cartridge in, and this was then fired by an external hammer. Operating the lever now extracted the empty case and loaded a fresh round. The rifle was fully stocked, with three barrel bands, and the foresight block doubled as a lug for the socket bayonet which fitted over the muzzle. There were also about 1000 built for the US Navy of which 700 have a large lug beneath the muzzle to locate and hold a sword bayonet. The Spencer was popular, because of its reliability and its power. Its maximum range was in excess of 2000 yards, and, according to one report, at 50 yards it would put its bullet through 13 inches of wood.

Another well-known carbine was the Sharps, and this too is covered in the cavalry section; but again the name also applied to an infantry rifle, though it is less well known than the carbine. About nine thousand Sharps rifles were purchased by the Union, and there are four distinct models. The basic version was the 'New Model 1859' which was the standard Sharps falling block breech, operated by a lever, with an external hammer dropping on to a cap nipple in the top of the breech block. This model had a lug for a sword-bayonet near the muzzle of the 30-inch barrel and was fully stocked. The 'New Model 1859' was also made with a 36-inch barrel, with a correspondingly longer fore-stock, and the sword-bayonet lug. The 'New Model 1863' returned to the 30-inch barrel and had no bayonet lug, while the 'New Model 1865' appears to have been similar to the 1863 but with a few minor manufacturing improvements.

The most technically advanced rifle to appear in the Civil War was probably the Henry lever-action repeater, of which 1731 were purchased by the Union at a cost of $63,953. The Henry was the successor to the early Volcanic, a lever-action design which used a novel cartridge which consisted of a hollow-based bullet, into the base of which was packed the propelling charge and percussion cap. The restricted space available for the charge inevitably meant that the Volcanic was a weak and inaccurate weapon, and Tyler Henry set about turning it into something more practical. Henry was a highly skilled gunsmith working

Below: The surplus Civil War weapons were converted for civil use after the war. This weapon began life as the Remington 'Zouave' percussion rifle of 1863 but has been converted after the war to breech-loading, using the Remington rolling block system.

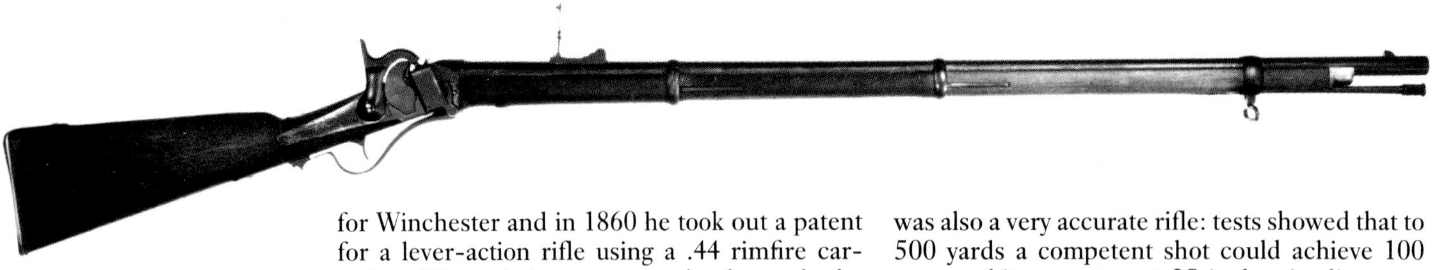

Above: An unusual Sharps rifle of 1855 made for the British Army for colonial use. A small number of these found their way back to America and were used in the war.

for Winchester and in 1860 he took out a patent for a lever-action rifle using a .44 rimfire cartridge. The tubular magazine lay beneath the barrel and was loaded from the front; the loader first withdrew the magazine spring to the front end of the tube and locked it there, then pivoted the end of the tube down so as to insert the cartridges. He then closed the tube and released the spring so as to force the cartridges back toward the breech.

The first cartridge moved on to a 'lifter', and when the under-lever was swung down this lifted the cartridge up and aligned it with the breech. Closing the lever forced the breech bolt forward and chambered the cartridge, leaving the external hammer cocked. Pulling the trigger dropped the hammer to fire the cartridge. Operating the lever again first extracted the empty case, then lifted up the next round and chambered it. The magazine held 15 shots, and an additional round could be loaded into the chamber so that the rifleman had 16 shots in hand, which could be fired at an impressive rate – 25 aimed shots a minute was within the capability of a well-trained soldier. Not for nothing did one Confederate soldier complain of 'that tarnation Yankee rifle that they load on Sunday and shoot for the rest of the week'. It was also a very accurate rifle: tests showed that to 500 yards a competent shot could achieve 100 percent hits on a target 25 inches in diameter, while at 1000 yards he could get the same result on a 48-inch diameter target.

For all that, Oliver Winchester found it hard going to interest the military in this rifle. The Chief of Ordnance, Brigadier-General Ripley, rejected the Henry and the Spencer rifles out of hand in 1861, and although (as related elsewhere) Spencer managed to get the approval of President Lincoln and have his rifles accepted into service, Winchester was not so fortunate, and had quite a struggle to get even the 1731 sold. At one stage of the struggle the Ordnance Department told the New Haven Arms Company that they would not accept the Henry rifle unless the company would arm a complete regiment, and keep it supplied with ammunition and replacement weapons, at its own expense. However, outside the principal military purchasing machine they were more successful and about ten thousand were sold directly to various state militia forces. The officers and men of the 66th Illinois Infantry actually bought their own rifles, at a cost of $50 each. The 7th Illinois Infantry and the 97th Indiana Infantry followed suit.

Right: Close-up of the breech of a Sharps sporting rifle (note the checkering, never seen on military rifles) with the breech block lowered.

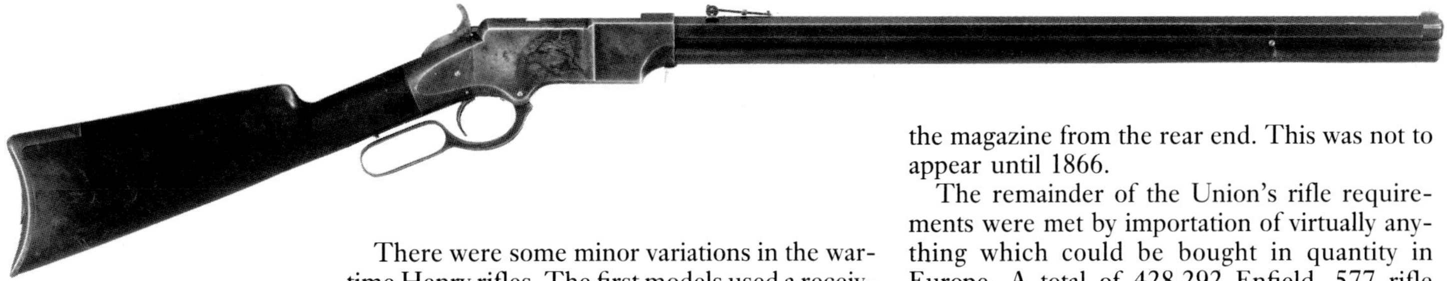

Above: A .44 Henry repeating rifle, an early model with case-hardened iron frame.

There were some minor variations in the war-time Henry rifles. The first models used a receiver made from wrought iron and had no positive means of latching the loading lever in the closed position. Then the receiver construction was changed to brass, and a securing latch for the lever was fitted underneath the stock. There were also changes in the shape of the butt-plate. All the Henry rifles had 24-inch barrels, and were distinguished by having no form of stock or fore end ahead of the receiver. It is also worth noting that none of the rifles made during the Civil War had the 'King Improvement' – the slot in the receiver which allowed the cartridges to be inserted into the magazine from the rear end. This was not to appear until 1866.

The remainder of the Union's rifle requirements were met by importation of virtually anything which could be bought in quantity in Europe. A total of 428,292 Enfield .577 rifle muskets were purchased in England as well as over 8000 short Enfield rifles. These were the British Army's Pattern 1853 (the long rifle) and the Short Sea Service rifle of 1858, numbers of which were also issued to British Army infantry regiments. The long rifle was of .577 caliber and rifled with three grooves, while the short rifle was of the same caliber but rifled with five grooves and a slightly tighter twist, which appears to have made the short weapon more accurate than the long. In appearance the Enfield rifle differed very little from its smooth-bored predecessor, and it

Below: Color Party of the 7th Illinois Infantry, Union Army, equipped with Henry repeating rifles, which appear to be the later brass frame model.

The Battle of Chattanooga: the Union charge led by General Thomas (right, with sword) to take Orchard Knob, 28 November 1863.

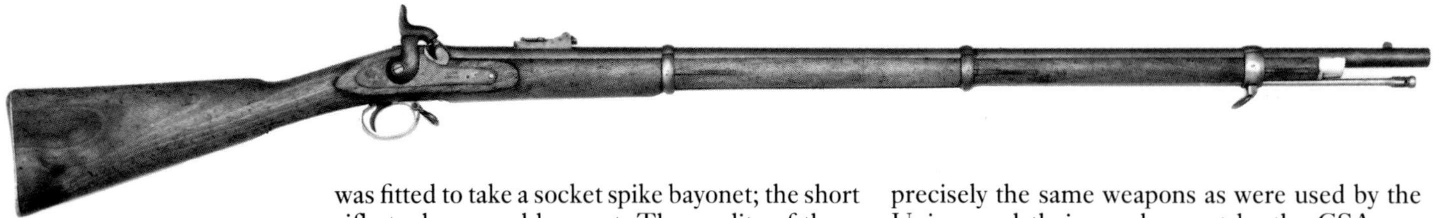

Above: The Enfield Rifle Musket, Pattern 1853, used and copied by the Confederate Army in large numbers.

was fitted to take a socket spike bayonet; the short rifle took a sword bayonet. The quality of these weapons varied; those manufactured at the Royal Small Arms Factory, Enfield (from where the weapon took its name), were uniformly excellent, but numbers were made by commercial gunmakers to the military specification but without the tight quality control which ensured interchangeability of parts and without the high quality of finish insisted upon by Enfield. Most of the commercially manufactured Enfields went to the Confederates, particularly those manufactured by the London Armoury Company.

Other foreign rifles included the Austrian .54 caliber Lorenz M1854, of which 226,000 were purchased; Belgian (57,400), French (44,250), Prussian (60,000), Prussian Jäger (29,850), Prussian commercial (30,000) and Italian (6000) rifles added to the total, and over 100,000 smooth-bore muskets were purchased from foreign sources, principally from Prussia and the various states of the German Confederation. Putting it mildly, the European countries were happy to unload all their obsolete and obsolescent weapons at seller's prices, so that they could use the money to re-equip with newer weapons – particularly the German states which wanted to outfit their men with the new Dreyse needle-gun. As one commentator put it: 'The refuse of all Europe passed into the hands of the American volunteers.' The rejection rate of these foreign-bought muskets, when they were inspected on their arrival in the United States, was extremely high. The official list of Union contract procurement ends with the catch-all item '641 rifles, various kinds, $15,256.78', and one is inclined to wonder what oddities are included in that sub-total.

Turning now to the Confederate Army, the 'Field Manual for the use of Confederate Officers on Field Duty' listed the US Rifle Musket Models 1842 and 1855 as being the CSA standard, plus the Rifle Model 1842 with the bore reamed out to .577 caliber. These were precisely the same weapons as were used by the Union, and their employment by the CSA was simply due to the fact that they existed in considerable numbers in the Southern states, the men were familiar with them, and they were constantly kept up to requirement by captured stocks.

In addition, of course, it was necessary to augment these with purchases and manufacture, and, true to form, some of the manufacture which took place in the South was in small quantities and of diverse design, depending upon what pattern could be obtained from which to copy or upon what the particular manufacturer fancied he was capable of doing. For example, the Asheville Armory, of Asheville, North Carolina, took the short Enfield rifle as their model and in 1862-63 made about three hundred weapons with 32.6-inch barrels. Similarly the two Cook Brothers, Ferdinand and Francis, who operated a plant in New Orleans, were Englishmen and, not surprisingly, also took the Enfield as their pattern, turning out copies of both the long and short rifles. Their operations in New Orleans were cut short by the approach of the Union Army and they removed their plant to Athens, Georgia, continuing to turn out rifles and carbines until 1864, several thousand weapons being made.

The Dickson, Nelson Company of Dawson, Georgia, busied themselves in 1864-65 with making a .577 rifle with a 34-inch barrel which was largely based on the US Model 1841 pattern. D C Hodgkins & Sons of Macon, Georgia, produced a small number of copies of the Springfield Model 1855 carbine in 1862-63, while the Tyler Ordnance Works of Tyler, Texas, produced several hundred copies of long and short Enfield and Austrian Lorenz rifle muskets between 1863 and 1865.

These, however, were the fringe manufacturers; the greater part of Confederate rifle production was carried out at three armories. The Fayetteville Armory of Fayetteville, North Caro-

Below: The Sharps & Hankins Model 1861 Navy rifle. A .52 caliber rimfire, operating the trigger-guard lever slid the barrel forward to open the breech.

Right: A contemporary engraving of an armorer repairing rifles and carbines.

lina, made several thousand copies of the US Model 1861 rifle musket using component parts captured at Harper's Ferry and later using parts manufactured entirely in the Armory. The early models, using captured parts, have a peculiar hump-backed lock plate, due to the fact that the plates were originally made for the Maynard tape priming system, but the addition of the Maynard system was either thought not worth the effort or, equally probably, sufficient parts for the Maynard device had not been captured. The locks are marked C.S.A. FAYETTEVILLE but carry no date. Once manufacture of locks began in the Armory, the lockplate was made without the hump and the lockplates had an eagle and the date added.

The Richmond Armory of Richmond, Virginia, made more rifles and carbines than any other Confederate factory, though the precise number turned out is not known. Again, the US Model 1861 rifle musket was used as the model, the

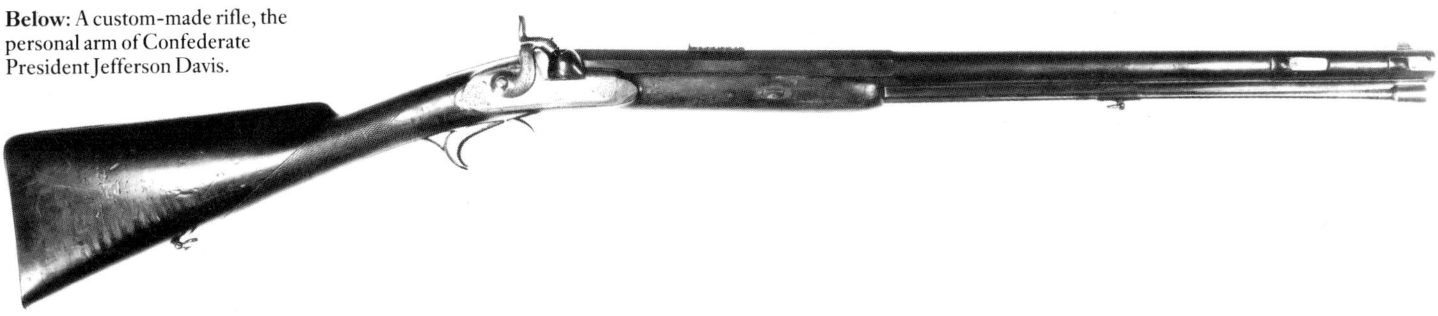

Below: A custom-made rifle, the personal arm of Confederate President Jefferson Davis.

Union soldiers pose at Appomattox Court House, April 1865.

Above: An engraving showing 'the Confederate Ordnance Armory, Charleston SC – Volunteer troops trying the arms.'

difference being that it was bored to .577 caliber, the Confederate standard. As with the Fayetteville Armory, first production of these weapons began by using parts and machinery taken from Harper's Ferry Armory in April 1861, and for this reason the Richmond guns also show the hump-backed lockplate. Once the tooling began to wear out, and new dies had to be made for the lockplates, Richmond shortened the hump. The markings on the lockplates vary but invariably include the word RICHMOND.

Three models were produced: a rifle with 40-inch barrel and three barrel bands; a 'musketoon' with 30-inch barrel and two bands; and a carbine with 25-inch barrel and two bands.

The third producer was the Palmetto Armory of Columbia, South Carolina. These weapons were actually manufactured before the Civil War on contracts issued by the State of South Carolina in 1852-53 and they were for either the Model 1841 US Percussion Rifle or the Model 1842 Percussion Musket. Since these weapons went, quite legitimately, into the South Carolina state armories, on the outbreak of war they became Confederate weapons. Except for their markings they are identical with the standard Union weapons.

Sniping Rifles

Sniping was carried out by both sides with considerable skill; perhaps the most famous were Berdan's Sharpshooters, every man of whom was required to obtain a group of ten shots within five inches of the bull's-eye at 200 yards' range before he could be admitted to the unit. But besides this and other specialist companies, almost every regiment had its snipers who were provided with the

Below: A double-barreled percussion shotgun of unknown make but with Remington locks. Shotguns were fairly commonly used, but were generally cut down to a more convenient length.

Right: Private Francis E Brownell of the 11th New York Infantry (the 'Fire Zouaves') of the Union Army. A good example of the ornate dress adopted by the 'Zouave' units.

A
12

Guardhouse and Guards of the 107th Colored Infantry, Union Army. The formation of 'Negro Regiments' was a contentious issue.

best rifles that could be procured. In general these were non-regulation heavy-barreled target or sporting rifles, often fitted with telescope sights. These sights were often as long as the rifle itself, since optical theory went little beyond the plain Galilean telescope at that time; they would doubtless display a pretty dim sight picture by modern standards, but in skilled hands, and with good light, they were formidable weapons.

Many of these rifles were provided with false muzzles to preserve the muzzle of the weapon from wear due to the passage of the ramrod. The rifle muzzle had three holes bored into the solid metal, and the false muzzle was a short piece of tube with three pegs which fitted these holes so that the tube formed an extension to the barrel. The cartridge and bullet were then introduced and rammed, and the false muzzle centered the bullet and took any abrasion from the ramrod. The sniper also made sure his bullets were of even weight and well formed, that his powder was of even granulation and perfectly mixed and dried, and he made a fetish of keeping the rifle clean.

Machine Guns

The Civil War was the first war in which machine guns were used, although their use was limited because of the scarcity of these weapons and because there was little understanding of how such weapons could be integrated into the tactical theories of the time. The idea of a gun which could be fired rapidly or which would discharge a volley of bullets was not new; experimenters had been trying such devices since the seventeenth century. The problem lay in the provision of ammunition for such a weapon, because as long as the round of ammunition consisted of a lead ball, a scoop of powder and a flint there was very

Left: Berdan's Sharpshooters skirmishing in a wheatfield during the Seven Days Battle.

Below left: 'California Joe,' one of the more famous marksmen who served with Berdan's Sharpshooters, with his Sharps rifle.

little way that repetition could be achieved. Once cartridges became self-contained and the percussion cap appeared there was another surge of interest, but again the need to integrate the loading of the cartridge and the positioning of the cap defeated any hope of making a practical weapon. It was not until metallic cartridges began to appear that success with a rapid-firing weapon could be considered feasible.

Nevertheless, the first machine gun to see any use in the Civil War, and, moreover, the one which was probably the most successful (because it was the simplest), was the Billinghurst-Requa Battery Gun, sometimes known as the 'Covered Bridge Gun'. Multiple firer it was; machine gun it wasn't. It was, in fact, an up-to-date version of an idea as old as artillery itself and which can be traced back to the fourteenth century – the Volley Gun or Ribaudequin.

Billinghurst was a renowned gunsmith from Rochester, New York, who had a high reputation for making sporting weapons of various types. Requa, of whom we know little, 'invented' the weapon, Billinghurst manufactured it. It consisted of nothing more than a row of 25 rifle barrels secured side by side on a wooden frame carried on a light wheeled carriage. Behind them was a slab of steel which contained 25 chambers and could be withdrawn from contact with the barrels by a lever. The 'breech' was opened and the chambers all loaded with powder and shot, either loose or in a paper cartridge. A groove in the breech block connected touch-holes leading to the 25 chambers, and a single percussion cap at one end of the groove fired a stream of powder trickled into the groove after the breech block had been closed. Thus the rate of discharge of the 25 barrels was proportional to the speed at which the string of powder burned its way across the breech block and the result was a ragged volley of 25 shots. After which the breech was opened and reloading commenced.

This was obviously a good weapon for short-range intensive fire, and it took its name of 'Covered Bridge Gun' from its aptness for mounting at one end of such a bridge to deny an enemy the chance of crossing. A volley from the Billinghurst-Requa, followed by a musket volley, then another volley from the Bridge Gun would soon persuade anyone that some other occupation was preferable to crossing bridges in the face of such fearsome firepower.

Below: The Billinghurst-Requa Volley Gun, on its wheeled carriage. The 25 barrels were loaded by operating the side levers to open the breech.

A rather more practical weapon was the Ager 'Coffee Mill' machine gun, so called from the feed hopper and the hand crank at the side, which resembled the coffee grinder of the period. The Ager had a special 'cartridge' which had to be prepared, in some quantity, before firing could begin. This was simply a steel tube, open at one end and fitted with a cap nipple at the other, into which a standard .577 caliber paper cartridge was loaded and a cap secured on the nipple. When sufficient of these had been made ready, firing could commence. One man placed handfuls of the cartridges into the hopper on top of the gun's receiver, while the gunner took aim and turned the hand crank. This withdrew the breech block, allowing one cartridge to fall from the hopper on to the feedway. As the crank turned so the cartridge was forced into the chamber and a hammer struck the cap to fire the charge. Further rotation opened the bolt, withdrew the empty tube and ejected it, and began loading the next. The discarded tubes were picked up and reloaded so that fire could be kept up, though it sounds as if more men would be required for reloading the cartridges than for actually operating the gun.

The Ager was offered to the Union Army, which promptly refused it. Political pressure was brought to bear with no avail, and eventually recourse was had to asking President Lincoln to rule on its acceptance. This he declined to do, never being one to interfere with the Army's decisions unless he felt he had good grounds, and in this case he claimed that his lack of military expertise rendered his opinion worthless. Eventually, however, as the war progressed, the Union authorities became a little more receptive to new ideas and 63 Ager guns were purchased at a cost of $53,485, though for some reason they were known officially as the 'Union Repeating Gun'. It is possible, although there is little evidence either way, that the cost – almost $850 per gun – was enough to deter the Union from buying any

Below: The .58 caliber Ager 'Coffee Mill' machine gun. This is the second gun to be built, and survives in remarkably good condition.

Right: A contemporary print of the 1865 model .50 Gatling gun.

more examples. After all, examples of the tried and tested 10-pounder cannon cost only $204.

The Confederate Army was far more alive to prospective new weapons than were the Union generals, and it was always ready to try anything which promised well. The Army had acquired a few Billinghurst-Requa guns, and also accepted an idea put forward by Captain Williams, a CSA army officer from Covington, Kentucky. The Williams 'One-Pounder' should, more properly, be considered almost as artillery in view of its 1.57-inch caliber, but it was a machine gun in concept so we can deal with it here.

A single-barreled weapon, the Williams was hand-operated and used a crank and connecting rod to force the breech block back and forward, in much the same manner as the Ager gun and, indeed, the later Gardner gun. As the gunner rotated the crank, his assistant dropped prepared paper cartridges into the breech and slipped a cap on to the nipple on the breech block. The movement of the crank then forced the cartridge into the breech and as the connecting rod came into position to form a solid strut behind the breech, so a hammer was tripped and fell on the cap to fire the shot. According to contemporary reports the Williams gun was capable of firing 65 shots a minute, but in view of the fact that the gunner's mate had to insert the cartridge and fix the cap for each shot, we can be excused for assuming that this was wishful thinking. A skilled pair might have got thirty rounds a minute out of it, and that would have been quite sufficient to produce a fearsome barrage of fire. Williams himself commanded a number of these guns in Pickett's Brigade, and they were used to good effect in the Battle of Seven Pines in May 1862.

The great missed opportunity in machine guns during the Civil War was, of course, the Gatling gun. Richard J Gatling was born in North Carolina; his father appears to have been an inventive man, devising a number of agricultural machines, and young Richard patented a machine for planting rice. After a short career selling his invention, he became a medical student and eventually qualified as a physician; he never went into practice and it has been averred that, being far-sighted, he merely took his degree in medicine so that he could better look after his family in times of epidemic.

Some time in the 1850s he first struck on the idea of a machine gun, and he took out his first patents in 1862. In order to solve the ammunition problem he took the idea of the pre-loaded steel tubular 'cartridge' from the Ager gun and applied this to a six-barreled weapon. One of the drawbacks of a fast-firing weapon was the heating effect of exploding several pounds of gunpowder in the barrel; the Williams gun suffered from this when fired for any length of time, the breech expanding and failing to seal properly. Gatling therefore arranged for his six barrels to rotate about a central spindle, with each barrel firing as it came to the six-o'clock position in its travel. For the remainder of the rotation it was either being loaded or having the empty tube extracted, and

Right: Richard Jordan Gatling, inventor of the immortal gun.

thus for five-sixths of its life it was cooling off between shots.

Gatling demonstrated his first gun at Indianapolis in 1862, and among the spectators was the Governor of Indiana, O P Morton, who was sufficiently impressed by the weapon to write to the Assistant Secretary of War to propose an official trial. Six guns were then manufactured by Miles Greenwood of Cincinnati, Ohio, but as they were nearing completion the factory caught fire and the guns and all the drawings were destroyed. Gatling then went to McWhinney, Ridge and Company, also in Cincinnati, and got them to make 12 guns in .577 caliber. But by this time he had discovered the rimfire principle and these guns were the first to be designed for a metallic cartridge, even though this cartridge was still pre-fitted into a steel tube which acted as the chamber of each barrel. The guns were sold, for $1000 each including 1000 cartridges, to General Benjamin Butler in Baltimore. Butler, for all that his reputation later suffered in New Orleans, was a percipient soldier and he put his Gatling guns to good effect during the Union's siege of Petersburg, Virginia.

Unfortunately, Dr Gatling was the victim of political uncertainty; in the first place he had been born in North Carolina, which made him a suspect Southern sympathizer, and in the second place, according to his critics, his choice of manufacturing in Cincinnati, on the edge of Union territory, was suggestive of a conspiracy by which Confederate raiders might cross the Ohio river at the appropriate time and capture any stock of Gatling guns which may have been manufactured to meet a Union order.

In 1864 Gatling severed his connection with McWhinney, Ridge and Company, moved to Philadelphia, and obtained the services of James M Cooper, a well-known gunsmith, to manufacture a totally new design. This dispensed with the steel-tube principle and loaded the rimfire cartridge into a chamber formed in the rear of each barrel. A helical cam drove each bolt forward in turn when it appeared at the upper position,

Right: A front view of the Gatling Gun showing the substantial carriage necessary to take it into battle.

Right: The ornate cast bronze nameplate on one of the original production Gatling guns.

chambering a cartridge. As the barrel moved down so the bolt was closed and the firing pin held cocked. At the lowest position in the rotation the firing pin was released, to fire the cartridge, and as the barrel began its move up the other side of the circle so the bolt was opened and the case extracted, ready to be reloaded when it reached the top.

This new design was tested by the Union Army in January 1865 and greeted with great enthusiasm. The Army suggested a one-inch caliber gun should be built, capable of firing ball bullets for long range work or buckshot bullets for close defence. Gatling set about building this and developing the necessary ammunition, and while he was thus engaged the Civil War ended. Eventually, in August 1866, the US Army formally approved of the Gatling and ordered the first 50 guns. Apart, therefore, from the 12 early models bought by Ben Butler, the Gatling never saw any application during the Civil War.

Hand Grenades

Grenades were an old invention which had more or less died out, but the Civil War revived them in new forms, principally because the invention of the percussion cap allowed the development of some ingenious methods of fuzing. Hitherto the only method of firing a grenade was to have a length of 'quickmatch' or blasting fuze hanging out of it, and light this prior to throwing it. As might be imagined, this was a hit-or-miss system and many grenades failed to operate because the fuze fell out or was extinguished in flight or on landing.

The standard 'grenade' of the early nineteenth century was simply a three-pounder or six-pounder cannon ball filled with gunpowder, with the fuze inserted in the neck and wedged there with a piece of rag or clay. These could be thrown, or, more generally, were simply dropped over the ramparts of forts when defenders were attempting to scale the walls. The British manual of ammunition of the period notes that 'men should be cautioned not to retain the grenade too long in their hands after lighting the fuze', a warning which we suspect would have been completely superfluous to any reasonably intelligent soldier.

Grenades of this nature reappeared during the Civil War, but more interesting are the specialized designs developed by the Union Army. Of these, Ketcham's grenade is perhaps the most well known. It consisted of a cast-iron oval head containing a charge of gunpowder to which was attached a short wooden tail rod carrying a set of pasteboard fins. The front end of the grenade was thickened and had a hole bored into it, terminating in a cap nipple which led into the gunpowder-filled interior. Into this hole fitted a short metal rod with a flat dished end which formed the nose of the grenade. When ready to be used, the nose rod was removed and a cap dropped in over the nipple, the rod then being replaced; it was held clear of the cap by a spring. The grenade was then thrown, the fins keeping it head-first in flight, and when it landed the rod was driven in to fire the cap and thus explode the gunpowder, shattering the grenade into lethal fragments. Ketcham's grenade was made in several sizes, the body weighing from one to five pounds, though the smaller sizes appear to have been more popular since they could be thrown further and with better accuracy. A total of 93,200 Ketcham's grenades were procured by the Union Army throughout the war.

The Haynes 'Excelsior' was typical of many ideas which seemed sound but failed to succeed in actual combat. It consisted of a sphere of cast iron filled with gunpowder and studded around its surface with 14 nipples. This all fitted into a second spherical container which unscrewed into two halves. The theory was that the soldier unscrewed the outer container, removed the inner sphere and crowned each nipple with a percussion cap. He then replaced it and screwed the outer sphere together, then threw the grenade. As might be imagined, no matter how the grenade fell one or more of the caps would be fired by the crushing effect of the inner sphere moving against the outer when the grenade suddenly stopped. The practical drawback was, of course, that priming the grenade in the face of an oncoming enemy was slow, and therefore it was advisable to prime a number of them and have them ready. If this was done, and some clumsy soldier happened to knock a primed grenade in passing, disaster followed. Even a careless throw could disturb the inner sphere sufficiently to fire the thing as it left the hand. A few experiences like that and the word got round that the 'Excelsior' was best left in its box and ignored.

Ammunition

The question of ammunition was a vexed one throughout the war and for both sides, since there grew up a multitude of calibers and chamberings so that almost every weapon demanded something slightly different. Periodically, particularly in the Union Army, there would be moves to standardize upon a limited number of calibers, but the quantity of weapons in service defeated every attempt, and it was not until the war was over and the oddball weapons cleared out of the inventory that anything approaching rationalization could be achieved.

The fundamental problem was, of course, to get a bullet into a muzzle-loading gun and ensure that when it came out again, under the influence of the powder charge, it bit into the rifling and spun. Engagement with the rifling was critical, too, since this ensured that all the gas evolved by the burning gunpowder actually got behind the bullet and pushed, rather than leaking past it.

There were two basic solutions: the *carabine à tige* system and the expanding bullet. In the former method the chamber of the weapon carried a central spigot or 'tige', which was formed by screwing in from the rear. When the powder charge was loaded, this dispersed into the space around the spigot. The ball was then dropped down the barrel and came to rest on top of the spigot. The ramrod followed, and a few sharp blows with the ramrod ensured that the soft lead bullet was deformed, spread slightly outwards so that the edge bit into the rifling grooves. When the charge was fired, the bullet was already engraved in the rifling, there was little or no leakage, and it picked up spin satisfactorily. The drawback to this system was that the area around the tige

Below: The Battle of Chickamauga; General Thomas' men holding the line against the Confederate troops of Braxton Bragg. Note how some of the soldiers in the rear ranks seem to be loading the rifles of their comrades in front.

Right: Female labor in an ammunition factory in Bridgeport, Connecticut.

was difficult to keep clean, the tige tended to corrode and eventually bend or break, and the varying power of the individual as he hammered down the rammer meant varying deformation of the ball and varying ballistic performance.

The expanding bullet system did away with any mechanical method of deforming the bullet and relied upon the explosion of the charge to do the job. The bullet itself, rather than being a simple ball, was now elongated, pointed at the front, and recessed in its base so as to leave a relatively thin lead skirt. The powder was loaded into the chamber, the ball was rammed down on top and that was that. On firing the charge, the first force of the explosion expanded the bullet skirt into the rifling and then it was expelled from the bore with spin.

The expanding bullet used in the Civil War by both sides was always called the 'Minie Ball' from the name of the French Army officer who invented it. Instead of merely relying on the gas pressure to work against the lead, Minie improved the basic idea (which was, in fact, due to William Greener the English gunsmith) by inserting an iron conical cup into a recess in the base of the bullet. This gave more positive expansion and better regularity. In fact he was over-insuring, as events showed. The British Army adopted the Minie bullet but eventually found there was a tendency for the iron cup to be blown out of the bullet, so they substituted a wooden plug and finally a clay one. Then came the Pritchett bullet for the Enfield rifle, which used no plug at all and went back to Greener's original

The Battle of Gettysburg: a somewhat romanticized engraving by Sartain.

idea of the soft lead skirt. All these variations appeared in American hands during the Civil War, but the Minie bullet was by far the most common, on both sides. The Union alone purchased over 46 million in .58 caliber.

The defect of gunpowder as a propelling charge was firstly the smoke it emitted, which soon turned battles into hazy affairs unless a stiff wind was blowing, and secondly the fouling it left behind in the rifling of the weapon. This fouling clogged the rifling grooves and eventually built up until it became difficult, then impossible, to ram the bullet into the barrel. Regular cleaning was the approved remedy for this, but regular cleaning was not always possible in the heat of battle. In an attempt to scour out the fouling, the Williams bullet was devised shortly before the war and, after passing tests in December 1861, it was approved for issue by the Union Army and three million were ordered. The Williams bullet resembled the Minie ball in general appearance but had a conical zinc washer held to its base by a lead disc and plug. On firing, the gas pressure drove the lead plug and disc forward to expand the zinc washer, forcing its edges out to scrape the sides of the bore. This scoured the fouling away as the bullet progressed; not all the fouling was removed, but intermittent use of a Williams bullet would keep the fouling down to a level where it no longer interfered with loading. Until close to the end of the Civil War every package of Union ammunition for the standard .58 rifles had one or two Williams bullet cartridges included among the Minie bullets. The cartridge with the Williams bullet was often identified by red or blue stained paper, but many soldiers threw them away since they claimed that the zinc washer damaged the rifling and the rifle lost its accuracy. This was never borne out by tests, which showed the Williams to be at least as accurate as the standard Minie ball. Some weapons, such as the Ager coffee-mill gun, used Williams bullets exclusively, since fouling in a fast-firing weapon was a serious defect.

The smooth-bore musket of pre-war days had been furnished with a 'buck and ball' cartridge, which contained a solid bullet and a number of smaller buckshot bullets, the idea being that if the principal bullet missed, the buckshot might do some useful damage. This type of loading was not

Below: A scene in the besieging trenches surrounding Petersburg, in the spring of 1865.

suited to a rifled weapon, so the 'Shaler' bullet was devised to replace it. This consisted of a round-nosed bullet with a hollow base, into which was fitted a second, conical bullet, also with a hollow base, into which went a third, solid-based conical bullet. This was loaded as a one-piece unit, held together by its paper covering, but split into three after firing.

Explosive bullets were employed in some numbers; this was before any conventions existed about 'humane bullets' – indeed, it was the use of explosive bullets during the Civil War which led to the Declaration of St Petersburg of 1868 outlawing explosive projectiles under 400 grammes in weight. The explosive bullet had been proposed in Europe well before the war, its principal military purpose being the attack on ammunition carts. In form it resembled a Minie ball but carried a copper tube in the nose, filled with fulminating composition or with gunpowder and a percussion cap. In 1863 the Union adopted the Gardner bullet, which had a copper tube cast into the center of the lead bullet, its mouth extending to the base of the bullet. The tube was filled with gunpowder, and the cavity in the rear of the bullet was then sealed with a paste of fine powder. This was ignited by the flash of the propelling charge and burned as the bullet flew through the air, until it finally ignited the main charge in the tube, exploding the bullet. The delay obtained by the powder paste was aimed at giving a burst at one and a quarter seconds after leaving the muzzle. Some accounts of the bullet refer to the track of smoke and sparks it left in the air, so that it apparently was a primitive form of tracer bullet, though this application was ignored.

Some 35,000 of these bullets, in .52, .58 and .69 caliber, were procured by the Union Army; 10,000 were used at Gettysburg, but another 10,000 were abandoned during a hasty move in Virginia and were captured by the Confederates. These were promptly turned against their former owners and fired back at the Union troops during the Battle of Vicksburg. Since the Union had not advertised their use of explosive bullets, this Confederate use was seized on by Northern newspapers and turned into an atrocity story, but investigations after the war showed the truth of the matter. Nevertheless, the Confederate Naval Laboratory at Atlanta appears to have copied the Gardner bullet and made about 40,000 'musket shells'. They were considered a dangerous projectile, since they were loaded with fulminate, and it is doubtful if many were ever used.

Whatever the weapon, loading at the muzzle demanded time and concentration. A trained soldier was expected to be able to get off three rounds in one minute, aimed fire; but in the heat and excitement of battle, fire was perhaps less well aimed than it might have been. Moreover, many poorly trained men appear to have been uncertain, in the roar of volleys, whether they had fired or not. It is a matter of record that after the Battle of Gettysburg over 27,000 muskets were collected from the battlefield. Upon examination, 24,000 of these were found to be loaded; of those, half had been loaded twice, 6000 were found to be charged with anything from three to ten loads and one actually contained 23 loads. The excitement was such that the soldier was loading, presenting the musket without firing – probably forgetting to place the cap on the nipple – then reloading and so on.

Above: The price of defeat. A Confederate soldier of Ewell's Corps, killed in a brief attack on 19 May 1864. A photograph by Timothy O'Sullivan.

Several of the specialized breech-loading weapons, particularly some of the patent carbines, demanded special ammunition. The Burnside carbine (discussed in the cavalry section) used a peculiar conical tinned brass or copper case with a thickened bulge just behind the bullet, so that it could be inserted base-first into the chamber of the gun. The base had a hole, sealed with paper or varnish, which admitted the flash from the percussion cap mounted on the gun's nipple.

The Gallagher cartridge also used a case loaded base-first, but this was a parallel-walled tube, again with a hole in the base and a bullet in the mouth. The Morse cartridge was a cylinder with a rim soldered to the bottom, and the bottom left open to take a rubber disc carrying a percussion cap. Many of these patent cartridges were made fairly robust so that they could be reloaded several times, given a supply of powder, caps and bullets.

3

ARTILLERY

Previous page: Troops of the 1st Connecticut Artillery at drill with 24-pounder garrison guns, Fort Richardson,Virginia, 1861.

The importance of artillery was recognized very early in the war. In August 1861, General Barry, Chief of Artillery of the Army of the Potomac, wrote to General McClellan:

> To insure success, it is of vital importance that the army should have an overwhelming force of field artillery. To render this more effective, the field batteries should, as far as possible, consist of regular troops.

What Barry really meant was that since the enemy they were fighting had very little in the way of naval power, the coast defense batteries could be raided for trained regular soldiers:

> With every disposition to do their best, the volunteer artillery do not possess the knowledge or experience requisite for thoroughly efficient service. I would therefore recommend that companies of regular artillery may be withdrawn from many of the forts on the Atlantic and Pacific seaboards and ordered to Washington at as early a date as practicable, to be mounted as field artillery.

He got his way and within a short time the Army of the Potomac had half the regular artillerymen of the US Army in its ranks as field gunners.

Shortly after this one field battery (A/2nd) was reorganized as horse artillery, the first horse artillery battery to be seen in the US Army since the Mexican War, and attached to the cavalry. It was soon to be followed by others as the utility of horse artillery was recognized.

What started Barry's concern was simply that when the Army of the Potomac was formed it had 50,000 infantry, less than 1000 cavalry, and 650 artillerymen manning 30 guns, organized into nine incomplete batteries. The organization of the period was such that batteries were loosely attached to infantry brigades, a system which was adequate for Indian wars and skirmishes but which, in a major battle, fragmented the artillery into small groups here and there under different command.

Barry and McClellan set about changing this; among Barry's first orders on reorganization were instructions that:

> The proportion of artillery should be in the ratio of at least two and a half guns to 1000 men, to be expanded, if possible, to three pieces . . . Each field battery to be composed, if practicable, of six, and none to have less than four guns, those of each battery to be of uniform caliber . . . The field batteries to be assigned to divisions . . . in the proportion of four to each division, one of which should be a regular battery, the rest volunteers, the captain of the regulars to command the artillery of the division . . . In the event of several divisions being united into an army corps, at least one half the divisional artillery to be withdrawn . . .

Right: Captain Horatio Gibson and the officers of his battery of Union Artillery, with a 12-pounder Napoleon, at Fair Oaks, Virginia.

and formed into a corps reserve . . . The reserve artillery of the whole army to consist of 100 guns comprising, beside a sufficient number of light mounted batteries, all guns of position and, until the cavalry be massed, all the horse artillery . . . The amount of ammunition to accompany the field batteries to be not less than 400 rounds per gun . . . A siege train of 50 pieces to be provided.

In point of fact, this was the first time a really systematic set of instructions for accompanying a field army had ever been promulgated in the US Artillery, largely because the US had never needed to put formations like army corps and divisions into battle before. However, like all organizations drawn up on a clean sheet of paper, Barry's, good as it was, could stand some improvement as experience was gained. After the Battle of Chancellorsville, therefore, the batteries of the division were removed and given to the army corps, and the batteries within each corps were then organized into brigades, thus making an even greater concentration of firepower.

The Confederates had seen the same light even earlier. Immediately after the Peninsula campaign in 1862 they began grouping their batteries in battalions, each with three to five batteries and a complete and well-thought-out administrative organization. This was in contrast to the Union Army which, blinded by tradition, ordained that 'as a general rule, artillery will be called for and received by batteries, thus rendering staff unnecessary . . .'. As a result, when the batteries were grouped into brigades no administrative staff was provided, and this had to be thrown together by raiding the batteries for their best officers, often leaving the actual command of the guns in the hands of juniors and those considered incompetent to perform the vital staff duties. The Confederates, appreciating the value of artillery, allowed a brigadier-general to every 80 guns, a colonel to every 40, a lieutenant-colonel to every 25; the Union Army, whilst agreeing that guns were a very good thing, left the command entirely in the hands of captains and majors, since it was thought that command of guns was not commensurate with the high responsibility of general officers. It was to be some time before the Union artillery commanders reached the rank of lieutenant-colonel.

It should be emphasized that in 1861 all artillery capable of going into the field with an army was horse-drawn; the distinction between horse and field artillery was simply that in the horse artillery every man was mounted, so that the bat-

Below: The Battle of Shiloh: Union artillery played a vital part in this, one of the bloodiest battles of the war.

Right: 'Bringing up the Guns', a painting by Gilbert Gaul. This well illustrates the difficulty of moving a 12-pounder in mud, though one suspects artist's license in depicting only two horses in the gun team.

tery could keep up with the cavalry in action, whereas in the field artillery many of the gun crews rode on wagons or marched alongside the guns, so that their speed of maneuver was less, being tied to the speed of the marching infantry. The US Army also had a third category – foot artillery; this was the name applied to those units which manned fixed defenses on the seacoast. A fourth category – mountain artillery – did not exist at the outbreak of war but was brought into being by the demands of some of the campaigns.

The standard artillery of the day was still the smooth-bore cast-iron or bronze gun, howitzer or mortar. In the 1860s the distinction between these three types was not quite as scientific as it was later to become, though it was well enough understood. The gun was for direct fire, against an enemy in plain view, and it fired a solid ball at what was for those days high velocity. The howitzer was for indirect fire, being aimed upwards at

Right: Union artillery at the Battle of Kenesaw Mountain, when an ill-advised attack by Sherman was thrown back with 3000 casualties.

Right: The 12-pounder Napoleon, virtually the standard field piece of both armies.

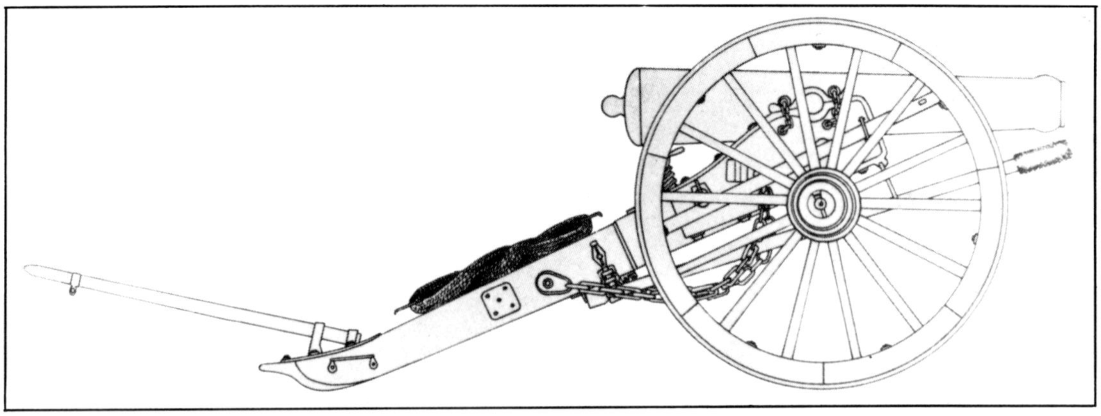

an angle, throwing its projectile high into the air so that it would fall steeply behind breastworks or walls, searching out an enemy in a defended position. Moreover, the howitzer usually fired an explosive shell which would burst at the target and spread fragments and destruction. The mortar was, in effect, a short and large-caliber howitzer; its principal difference was that it could *only* fire at high angles, whereas the howitzer could, if the occasion warranted, be depressed to fire at low angles in the direct role.

The standard US artillery at the outbreak of war consisted of 6-pounder and 12-pounder field guns, 12-, 24- and 32-pounder field howitzers; 12-, 18- and 24-pounder siege guns, eight-inch and 24-pounder siege howitzers, eight-inch, 10-inch and 24-pounder siege mortars; and 32-pounder and 42-pounder coast defense guns, eight-inch and 10-inch Columbiad coast guns, eight-inch and 10-inch coast howitzers, and 10-inch and 13-inch coast mortars. All these were cast-iron or cast bronze smooth-bore guns, but the War Department had been experimenting with different systems of manufacture and with rifled artillery for some years. Early in 1860 plans were made for converting half the existing artillery to rifled guns by the 'James Conversion', a method of cutting rifling into existing smooth-bores, but, as was found by every other country which tried it, this was not a practical system; it weakened the guns and, since the object of a rifled gun was, among other things, to allow it to fire a heavier shot, the result was usually an explosion which wrecked the gun. However, one

Below: Union gunners at drill with a Parrott 10-pounder field gun.

Right: Officers of the 2nd US Artillery with a 3-inch Ordnance Rifled Muzzle Loading gun.

improvement had been a success; the War Department had acquired the drawings and specification of a new 12-pounder French gun which had been designed by Napoleon III. His idea had been to develop a gun which would replace, in a single piece, some of his light and heavy weapons. The US Army appreciated his reasoning and adopted the 'Napoleon' in 1857,

Right: The odd-looking 900-pounder Wiard Gun, an experimental design. Note the intricate casting, intended to strengthen the barrel but save weight at the same time. It was not a success.

Above: Union 13-inch Siege Mortars, outside Yorktown in April 1862.

nominating it a 'gun-howitzer', not from its ability to reach great elevation but from the fact that it could fire shot or shell.

With the split which followed Secession, specimens of all these guns found their way into both the Union and Confederate Armies, so that in the early days both sides were using much the same weapons. However, as the war progressed and the demand for more and more artillery grew, both sides were forced on to the open market to obtain whatever they could. This opened the door to a number of inventors and factories who, in peacetime, would perhaps never have given much thought to artillery manufacture; nor, had they done so, would they have had much chance of interesting the Army in their products. But with the unsatisfied armies of both sides demanding guns, a wide selection of weapons appeared; and since the time was ripe, much of this accretion was of rifled guns. The other side of the coin was that many of these inventors and manufacturers had also designed special ammunition to fit their brainchildren, which presented some logistic problems. As an example, Rosecrans's Army in February 1863 mustered 32 6-pounder smoothbores; 24 12-pounder howitzers; eight 12-pounder Napoleons; 21 James rifled guns; 34 10-pounder Parrott guns; two 12-pounder Wiard steel guns; two 6-pounder Wiard steel guns; two 16-pounder Parrott guns; and four 3-inch rifled 'ordnance' guns.

There is little doubt that those rifled and breech-loading guns which did get into Union service did so against considerable official opposition. The Report of the Joint Congressional Committee on Ordnance of 1869 reviewed the

Right: A Union 12-pounder battery at Gettysburg.

Above: A Confederate coast defense battery outside Charleston, SC. The gun in the foreground is an 8-inch Columbiad smooth-bore.

performance of the Ordnance Department during the war and was extremely critical:

The difficulty appears to have been twofold; first, the ordnance officers, knowing their positions secure to them for life, have not felt the incentive to exertion and improvement which stimulates men not in government employ, and they have become attached to routine and to the traditions of their corps, jealous of innovation and new ideas and slow to adopt improvements. An illustration of this is found in the fact that the late war was fought with muzzle-loading guns, although a variety of excellent breech-loaders were urged upon the attention of the government constantly. In the second place, these officers ... came to look upon themselves as possessing all the knowledge extant upon the subject of ordnance, and regarded citizen inventors and mechanics who offered improvements as ignorant and designing persons ... Another difficulty that has retarded progress ... has been the fact that prominent officers have been inventors of arms and have possessed sufficient influence to secure the adoption and retention in service of their inventions, frequently without due regard to the question of real merit, and to the prejudice of other and better devices brought forward by citizens or developed in other countries...

The most common gun was the light 6-pounder, a simple muzzle-loader mounted upon a wooden two-wheeled 'stock trail' carriage. The stock trail was still considered relatively new;

Right: Union gunners with 18-pounder siege guns in an unidentified fort.

prior to about 1835 all American artillery used the 'flask' trail, an open frame of timber composed of two substantial side pieces joined by transoms. This had been used since the earliest days of artillery, but in the latter half of the seventeenth century the British and French had adopted the stock trail, in which the trail of the carriage was simply one solid piece of wood. This reduced the weight, made the carriage easier to manhandle and gave sundry other manufacturing advantages. Although the official American story (as in Birkheimer's *Historical Sketch of the US Artillery*) is that the idea was adopted from the French, in fact the US Army captured a number of British stock trail guns during the war of 1812 and it was this which led them to begin experiments. But it was not until 1836 that the stock trail was officially adopted, and by the outbreak of the Civil War it had completely replaced the old flask trail.

The next most common, probably the most important and certainly the most celebrated was the Light 12-pounder Model 1857, or the 12-pounder Napoleon. As noted above, the details of this weapon were acquired from France, and it fitted well into the existing system since the US Army needed a gun somewhat heavier than the 6-pounder but not as ponderous as their existing 12-pounder Model 1841. The weight of the Napoleon was designed to be 100 pounds of metal per pound weight of shot, and it actually weighed 1227 pounds; the Model 1841 had weighed 1757 pounds. (Note that this was the weight of the gun alone, excluding the weight of the carriage.) The Model 1841 had been 78 inches long, the Napoleon was 66 inches long; a lighter gun meant a slightly less substantial carriage, so that whereas the M1841 carriage had weighed 1175 pounds. that of the M1857 weighed 1125. Both fired the same 12.3-pound shot, but the lighter and shorter gun developed somewhat less velocity so that its range for a given elevation was less; at five degrees elevation the M1841 sent its shot to 1665 yards, while at the same elevation the Napoleon ranged to 1620 yards.

The Napoleon was cast of bronze. This had been the standard gun metal since artillery manufacture had begun, though there had been, from time to time, experiments with cast iron; indeed for some years all new cannon had been made of iron. Unfortunately many of these had resulted in failures and cast iron came to be officially regarded as a second best. But in 1840 Mr Poinsett, Secretary of War, decided to haul the US artillery into the present day; he had received a report

Below: Contemporary engraving of the attack on Fort Sumter, 13 April 1861.

Right: The 'Table of Fire' for the Light 12-pounder field gun, showing the range and the time of flight from firing to impact for three types of projectile; the time is only given for shell and spherical case (shrapnel), since it was the fuze-setting data and was irrelevant in the firing of solid shot.

TABLE OF FIRE. LIGHT 12-POUNDER GUN. MODEL 1857.

SHOT. Charge 2½ Pounds.		SPHERICAL CASE SHOT. Charge 2½ Pounds.			SHELL. Charge 2 Pounds.		
ELEVATION In Degrees.	RANGE In Yards.	ELEVATION In Degrees.	TIME OF FLIGHT. Seconds.	RANGE In Yards.	ELEVATION In Degrees.	TIME OF FLIGHT In Seconds.	RANGE In Yards.
0°	323	0°50′	1″	300	0°	0″75	300
1°	620	1°	1″75	575	0°30	1″25	425
2°	875	1°30′	2″5	635	1°	1″75	615
3°	1200	2°	3″	730	1°30′	2″25	700
4°	1325	3°	4″	960	2°	2″75	785
5°	1680	3°30′	4″75	1080	2°30′	3″5	925
		3°40′	5″	1135	3°	4″	1080
					3°45′	5″	1300

Use SHOT at masses of troops, and to batter, from 600 up to 2,000 yards. Use SHELL for firing buildings, at troops posted in woods, in pursuit, and to produce a moral rather than a physical effect; greatest effective range 1,500 yards. Use SPHERICAL CASE SHOT at masses of troops, at not less than 500 yards; generally up to 1,500 yards. CANISTER is not effective at 600 yards; it should not be used beyond 500 yards, and but very seldom and over the most favorable ground at that distance; at short ranges, (less than 200 yards,) in emergency, use double canister, with single charge. Do not employ RICOCHET at less distance than 1,000 to 1,100 yards.

CARE OF AMMUNITION CHEST.

1st. Keep everything out that does not belong in them, except a bunch of cord or wire for breakage; beware of loose tacks, nails, bolts, or scraps.
2d. Keep friction primers in their papers, tied up. The pouch containing those for instant service must be closed, and so placed as to be secure.
Take every precaution that primers do not get loose; a single one may cause an explosion. Use plenty of tow in packing.

(This sheet is to be glued on to the inside of Limber Chest Cover.)

from the Board of Ordnance averring that bronze was to remain the standard material, though experiments with iron would continue. This was not good enough for the Secretary:

> Judging by the experiments reported by the Board it appears certain that iron is abundantly strong, and that if guns sometimes fail it is not because the gun is of iron but because the gun-founder is not perfect in his art. At present he makes a good gun by accident, whereas it is by accident only he should make a bad one.

Poinsett also brought out a vital economic point:

> We possess the best quality of iron; but copper is not found or wrought in sufficient quantities, and tin not at all; and it is important that the armament of our navy, fortifications and troops should be drawn from an independent source . . . The partial use of bronze is not objected to, but the Board of Ordnance must apply itself to acquire a sufficient knowledge of the subject to cast the guns within our own arsenals, as this Department is not satisfied with those that have hitherto been made in private foundries.

This stung the Board of Ordnance, but the Secretary had his way, and intensive work began on developing sound cast-iron guns, a program which paid off with some remarkably good weapons in time for the Civil War. The most important development in this program was the invention, by Captain Thomas J Rodman, of a method of casting an iron smooth-bore gun around a water-cooled core, so that the metal forming the inner surface of the barrel cooled and hardened first to give a very wear-resistant surface. The remainder of the metal cooled down more slowly and, in so doing, compressed the inner metal so as to give the gun additional strength to resist the explosion of the cartridge. Rodman began experimenting in the late 1840s, and by the late 1850s had perfected his system to such a high degree that in a trial conducted by the War Department six ordinarily cast guns lasted a total of 772 rounds before being worn out or blowing up, whilst six Rodmans fired 5515 rounds between them and were still considered serviceable. In 1859 the Department ordered that henceforth all larger types of gun would be cast on the Rodman system.

Another system of construction was devised by Robert P Parrott, manager of the West Point Iron Foundry, near Cold Spring, New York. He first cast a gun, either in the conventional manner or by using Rodman's system, but he then made a wrought-iron tube or 'hoop' which was heated until it expanded, then slipped over the breech end of the cast-iron gun and allowed to cool and contract. This gave the breech and chamber additional strength without adding as much weight as would have been required in a pure cast

Above: A bronze 12-pounder Napoleon, beautifully preserved as a museum exhibit and provided with all its 'sidearms.'

gun. Instead of forming his guns on a gentle taper, as had always been done, Parrott, a typical nineteenth-century pragmatist, simply left the rear end of the gun thicker, so that his designs can easily be recognized by the sudden and angular change in diameter.

As these improved guns appeared, there was some concern that the existing iron and bronze guns might be rendered obsolete overnight, and since they represented a very high proportion of the existing artillery there was a search for some method of improving them so that they could continue to serve. Among the many ideas put forward was the 'Brooke' gun, which simply took an existing cast weapon and turned down the breech section to a smooth surface, then shrank a wrought-iron hoop round it to add strength.

The smooth-bore gun had some intrinsic drawbacks, all of which were well known. In the first place the smooth-bored gun could only fire a round ball; any attempt at firing an elongated projectile simply resulted in its turning end-over-end as it flew through the air, and destroyed any hope of accuracy. Secondly, the round ball governed the weight of projectile; given a gun of specific caliber there was one and only one ball which would fit, which is why the guns of the day were usually known by the weight of shot they fired and not by their caliber. Thirdly, accuracy was poor because the ball was a poor fit in the bore; it had to be, since if it was a tight fit it would be almost impossible to ram it down into the cannon, because of the air trapped inside the bore. Some of this would, it is true, escape from the vent above the chamber, but very slowly, and once powder fouling built up loading would become impossible. The ball had to have 'windage' – the difference in diameter between the interior of the bore and the exterior of the ball – in order to be loaded; and when the gun was fired, a lot of the explosion gas, which should have been pushing the shot up the barrel, actually leaked past it through the windage and was wasted. Since the ball was not a tight fit it bounced from

Above: The breech of a 12-pounder Armstrong rifled breech-loader, with the vent-piece partly withdrawn. The brass device above the breech screw is the rear sight, graduated and adjustable to compensate for cross-winds.

Right: A section of the barrel of an Armstrong rifled gun, together with two shells, showing the lead coating before, and, marked with the rifling pattern, after firing.

side to side inside the bore as it was fired, and its direction depended upon which side it bounced last before leaving the muzzle.

All these things had been known for many years, and theorists had seen that the solution to most of the troubles was the adoption of rifling. Cutting spiral grooves in the gun and so bestowing twist upon the shell brought many advantages. The shell could be made longer and given a better shape for passing through the air, because once the shell was spun it took on the same sort of stability as a gyroscope and resisted any attempt – by wind, for example – to push it off course. The shot, being bigger than a simple ball, could be heavier, thus doing more damage at the target. And fouling would tend to concentrate in the grooves, giving a longer time before it interfered with loading. The principal advantage, however, was simply that the elongated shell passed through the air with less resistance than the ball, and, since the adoption of rifling usually decreased the windage so that the gas was employed

Right: A 15-inch Rodman gun, providing part of the defenses of Washington DC.

more efficiently, rifled guns promised increased power and greater range.

The practical difficulty was that the gun still had to be loaded from the muzzle, so that the shot had to be capable of being pushed down the bore easily, but had somehow to grip the rifling on the way out.

The first practical solution appeared in France in the 1840s when Colonel Treuille de Beaulieu proposed cutting three helical grooves in a gun barrel and employing a shot carrying a row of three studs on its body. The cartridge was loaded into the gun and rammed into the chamber, then the shot was presented to the muzzle, base-first, so that the studs entered the three grooves. As the shot was rammed, it turned under the influence of the studs riding in the helical grooves, and when the cartridge was fired the shell was blown out, again rotating due to the studs riding in the grooves. The US Army began experiments with this system in 1855 but had made little progress by the time the war began. Their principal search was, again, for a convenient method of adapting existing guns, and this was done by the method

Right: A 9-pounder Whitworth rifled breech-loader, showing the hexagonal projectiles below the trail.

Above: A Confederate coast defense battery at Fort Fisher, Wilmington, with an imported British Armstrong 150-pounder rifled muzzle-loading gun.

advocated by Colonel James, simply taking existing cast bronze guns, smoothing the bores and cutting the requisite grooves into them. The fundamental defect of this was that since the object in view was to fire heavier projectiles, it inevitably led to the guns being overstrained in use, though it took time for this to make itself apparent. As a result there were a number of 'James Rifles' in use on both sides during the early part of the war.

An alternative to the groove-and-stud system was to use ribs on the shot, these being angled to suit the twist of the rifling grooves. Another alternative was to do away with grooves and shape the entire interior of the bore, manufacturing the shot to conform. This was the system advocated by Lancaster and Whitworth, two eminent English engineers, both of whom built guns on this principle. The Lancaster was the first, and a small number had been sent to the Crimea with the British expeditionary force in 1854. The bore of the Lancaster gun was oval in section, instead of being round, and the oval twisted from chamber to muzzle. The shot was also oval, with the sides planed to match the angle of twist. The shot was rammed in from the muzzle, and when it was fired it followed the pitch of the twisted oval to take up spin. At least, it did in theory. In practice the Lancaster was prone to jamming the oddly shaped shot in the bore either when being rammed or when being fired, damaging the surface of the bore and firing inaccurately. The British Army rejected the idea, but Lancaster persisted and a handful of his guns found their way to the Confederate Army during the war.

The Whitworth principle was similar, except that Whitworth made his bore hexagonal, and then twisted it. Similarly the shot was hexagonal, and it followed the twist when fired so as to obtain the necessary spin. The Whitworth system was rather better than the Lancaster, but careless handling could also jam the shot.

The most successful rifled gun in the world at the time was undoubtedly the English Armstrong gun. This had been devised by William Armstrong, a lawyer turned hydraulic engineer, after studying reports of the Crimean War. He was struck by the fact that a standard cast muzzle-loading gun firing an 18-pound shot weighed over three tons, and he decided to examine gun construction to see if it was possible to produce a powerful gun without the excess weight. He invented a system of 'building up' a gun, using a rifled wrought-iron barrel and then shrinking additional wrought-iron hoops around it so as to build up strength where it was needed – principally over the chamber. The hoops, shrunk one upon another, gave the gun compressive strength to withstand internal pressures. He then rifled the gun with a number of narrow and shallow grooves, and devised a shell coated with lead. Finally, he arranged for the gun to be loaded at the breech end, and not from the muzzle.

Armstrong's breech-loading system was, by modern standards, somewhat cumbersome, but for the 1860s it was a revelation. The gun was bored through from one end to the other, and a square vertical slot was cut into the gun body, about a foot from the rear end. In front of this slot the chamber was formed, somewhat larger in diameter than the bore of the gun, and from this the rifled portion began. Behind the slot the bore was screw-threaded, and into it went a massive hollow steel screw with a weighted arm which allowed it to be screwed in and out. The slot was filled with a square block of metal known as the 'vent-piece', because it carried the usual sort of ignition vent, and it was provided with a handle so that it could be lifted in and out of the top of the slot.

To load, the screw was given a half turn to loosen it and the vent-piece lifted out. The shell was then inserted into the tubular centre of the screw and rammed across the slot and into the gun, where the lead coating on the shell bit into the rifling. The gunpowder charge, wrapped in a cloth bag, was then rammed through the screw and into the chamber. The vent-piece was dropped back into the slot and the screw turned to tighten against the vent-piece, forcing it up against the back end of the chamber. The vent-piece had a facing of copper which formed a gas-tight seal when the screw was properly tightened. A 'friction primer' was inserted into the vent; this was a goose-quill filled with gunpowder and with a topping of match composition, through which ran a jagged steel pin, ending in a loop. The gunner hooked a lanyard into the loop and jerked the pin out of the primer; this friction caused the match composition to inflame, lighting the gunpowder, which flashed down the vent and fired the gunpowder cartridge. The explosion drove the shell into the bore, causing the lead coating to engrave completely into the rifling, and out went the shell, spinning.

According to tests carried out in England when the Armstrong was first introduced, its accuracy was something like fifty times that of a conventional smooth-bore gun, and it could out-range any weapon of comparable size with ease. Moreover Armstrong had, in modern terms, developed a 'weapon system', since he had produced an explosive shell and a time fuze to accompany the weapon, ensuring that the utmost utility was extracted from his design.

Whitworth almost immediately attempted to compete with Armstrong by developing a breech-

Below: Artillery units under fire during Pickett's charge at the Bloody Angle, Gettysburg, 3 July 1863.

Above: A Union siege battery outside Atlanta.

Below: Sheridan's final charge at Winchester, Virginia, on 19 September 1864; this defeat of the Confederates opened the Shenandoah valley for the Union Army.

loader. His method of breech closing was closer to modern-day technology than Armstrong's, but it failed to prosper. His gun was bored all the way through and ended in a chamber, just as Armstrong's did, but he stuck to his twisted hexagonal rifling system. The outer surface of the gun body, around the chamber aperture, was formed with lugs, and a hinged cap could be swung around so as to fit over the rear of the gun and, turned half a turn, lock its interrupted lugs into the lugs on the gun. A copper plate inside the breech cap was forced tightly against the mouth of the chamber, since when the cap was rotated there was a slight pitch to the gun lugs which pulled the cap tightly against the gun body. A friction primer was inserted into a vent in the cap and fired in the same way as the Armstrong gun. One advantage which the Whitworth had over the Armstrong was that if necessary the breech cap could be left closed and the gun loaded from the muzzle, impossible with the Armstrong due to the lead coating on the shells. Why anyone would want to do this is an open question, but Whitworth's supporters always made a big point of it.

What this eventually amounted to was that there were three different approaches to the matter of rifling which had all been tried and tested: the few large grooves of the rifled muzzle-loading system; the multiple fine grooves developed by Armstrong; and the 'mechanical fit' using a twisted bore as adopted by Whitworth and Lancaster. These appeared to have exhausted the possibilities, and anyone attempting to make a rifled gun in the 1860s, whether muzzle- or breech-loaded, adopted one of the three. The Blakely gun, numbers of which were bought in England by both sides, used six deep grooves and a studded shot; Parrott adopted multi-groove

Above: Union artillery moving into position during the Battle of South Mountain, September 1862, as McClellan advanced cautiously into Virginia.

rifling and had to devise some method of loading his shell easily but making it spin when it came out. But more of this when we discuss artillery ammunition.

The field artillery was the artillery of maneuver, the artillery which accompanied the marching troops or the cavalry and gave them direct support in battle. But when, as often happened, the advancing troops ran up against some strong defenses, heavier guns were needed, and here the siege artillery came into play.

The governing factor in siege artillery was the weight which could be pulled behind a team of horses; indeed this was the governing factor in any artillery, but the size of the team differed. Field and horse artillery used a six-horse team, which set the weight limit at about 3300 pounds; siege artillery moved more slowly and used teams of up to ten horses, so they could go just over 10,000 pounds. The heaviest movable piece of siege artillery was the 24-pounder smooth-bore gun. This fitted on a stock trail carriage which was similar to that of a field piece but bigger, and in order to move it the trail was lifted and pinned to a limber, a pair of wheels with a cross-axle, arranged for horse draught. The gun was prepared for movement by opening the capsquares, the curved metal plates which kept the gun trunnions in their bearings in the carriage, and then the gun itself was prised back with handspikes until the trunnions dropped into a second set of bearings further back on the carriage cheeks. This moved the center of gravity back, so balancing the weight between the four wheels of the gun and limber. The all-up weight was 10,155 pounds, just within the capabilities of a ten-horse team.

The 24-pounder was a 'battering gun', capable of hurling its ball through thicknesses of earth parapet or stone walls at considerable ranges. It was generally accompanied by the eight-inch smooth-bore howitzer, carried on a similar type of limber carriage. The name 'eight-inch' indi-

Right: The aftermath of Sedgwick's assault at Marye's Heights, 3 May 1863. A Confederate caisson and gun team destroyed by a shot from the 2nd Massachusetts Artillery. The man leaning against the tree stump is General Herman Haupt.

cates that this was a shell-firing gun – only shot-firing weapons were called 'pounder'. The howitzer was able to fire powder-filled shells over obstacles to give anti-personnel and incendiary effects at the target.

For even greater effect, particularly where the target was well fortified and defended, siege mortars could be brought up. These were short, stubby weapons on a very simple carriage consisting of little more than two sides and connecting transoms. They were carried on flat wagons; to place the mortar in action the wagon was drawn to its site, then the front wheels and axle were removed and the bed of the wagon was lowered to the ground. The mortar and its carriage were then slid down the wagon to the ground and the wagon was removed. The mortar carriage was usually emplaced on a prepared 'bed' of timber, giving it a smooth working platform and also spreading the recoil force so that the mortar did not gradually subside into the ground. Since the barrel was always at 45-50 degrees elevation it was not possible to aim in the normal way. The gunner stood behind the mortar with a length of

Right: Union battery No. 4 of 13-inch mortars outside Yorktown, 1862.

Above: A Union mortar battery preparing its position at Dutch Gap. After excavating and levelling platforms, the carriages will be set upon balks of timber and the barrels manhandled into position on the carriages.

cord and a plumb-bob, which he held in front of his eye so that the cord hung in front of the target. He then had the crew heave the mortar sideways until a line marked down the center of the mortar was aligned with the plumb-line. That took care of the direction; the range was determined simply by altering the amount of powder in the cartridge. The gunner would have a table of ranges and powder weights, and having estimated the range to the target would weigh out the correct charge and load it. The projectile was then loaded into the bore and the mortar fired either by a hot match applied to the powder-filled vent, or by the new friction primer. The gunner would observe the fall of the shot and make adjustments to the powder weight accordingly, until he hit the target.

The mortar generally fired hollow shell, filled with gunpowder or with incendiary composition, the object being to do as much damage as possible. Mortars were often employed to attack the buildings and installations behind the defenses; the howitzers and guns hammered the fortifications, while the mortars pounded the rear area, setting fires and destroying matériel.

Although the Chief of Ordnance had raided the seacoast fortresses for trained artillerymen at the outbreak of war, the Confederates soon began naval operations of various sorts, and it became necessary to keep the coast defenses in operation, manning them largely with volunteers. Moreover, several forts had to be constructed on the Mississippi and other rivers, by both sides, to

Above: Battery Rogers, on the Potomac River, with a 100-pounder Parrott gun in the foreground and a 10-inch Columbiad behind.

defend their furthest domains, and these had to be armed because of the variety of gunboats prowling around on the inland waterways.

The coast defense gun was 'artillery of position' – once installed it tended to stay there, because even if a field army had cast greedy eyes at it, the average coast gun was far too ponderous to be moved. The smallest coast artillery piece was the 32-pounder smooth-bore gun, the barrel alone weighing over three tons, while the largest was the 20-inch Rodman smooth-bore which weighed 52 tons and fired a half-ton shot. Between these two extremes were a range of seven-, eight-, 10- and 15.75-inch smooth-bores, and five-, six-, eight-, 10- and 12.75-inch rifled guns of various makes. Many of these latter rifled weapons – the 80-pounder Whitworth, the eight-inch and 12.75-inch Blakelys, the 150-pounder Armstrong – could hardly be called 'standard' since they represented a handful of guns which their designers had made simply to show what they were capable of doing, and since both the Union and the Confederacy needed coast defense guns they soon found buyers. The more official weapons, on the Union side, were the 100-pounder, 200-pounder and 300-pounder Parrott rifles, while both sides used whatever heavy smooth-bores they could find.

Coast defense guns were mounted on 'seacoast carriages' which were two-piece assemblies of a carriage and a slide. The carriage resembled the upper part of a field carriage with the trail; in

Above: The Union artillery park at City Point, Virginia, in 1864, with a fine collection of different guns and mortars awaiting issue.

other words two side cheeks supporting the gun, joined by transoms and with some form of elevating mechanism to move the gun up and down. This sat on top of the slide, a long wooden staging which was anchored to a pivot in the ground at its front end and carried on a set of truck wheels at the rear. These wheels were at right angles to the axis of the slide, so that the rear end of the slide could be rolled round on a circular path, pivoting around the pintle at the front end. The truck wheels generally sat on a curved iron strip known as the 'racer' which was let into the masonry of the fortress rampart.

The gun carriage carried a pair of wheels set on an eccentric axle so that they could be lifted up, allowing the carriage to sit squarely on the slide,

Above: Firing a Sawyer rifled muzzle loading cannon from Fort Calhoun against Confederate batteries on Sewell's Point, near Norfolk, Virginia.

or lowered so as to raise the rear end of the carriage. To load, the carriage wheels were lowered and the entire carriage and gun hauled back along the slide until the muzzle was clear of the parapet and the crew could get round it to load. After the gun had been loaded, handspikes were used to lever the carriage forward again until it was positioned at the front end of the slide, with the wheels withdrawn and the barrel poking out over the fortifications. The gun was pointed by moving the entire slide from side to side around the front pivot, and elevated for range by means of a screw or by wedges and handspikes. When the gun fired, the entire gun and carriage slid backwards on the surface of the slide, and this recoil movement was controlled, to some extent, by the friction of the slide's movement. It could be decreased, when heavy charges were in use, by sprinkling sand on the surface of the slide or, for reduced charges, increased by a layer of grease. The object was to have the carriage recoil to a fixed point every time so that it could conveniently be reloaded.

This hit-and-miss system was then improved, at about the time of the Civil War, by the invention of the 'compressor'. A sheaf of iron plates was suspended beneath the carriage, into a gap in the body of the slide; arranged in this gap was another sheaf of iron plates, so that the carriage plates were in between the slide plates. A screw jack could be operated to tighten the carriage plates against the slide plates, so that when the carriage recoiled it had to drag its plates through those of the slide, damping down the recoil movement. By adjustment of the screw jacks, the tension could be regulated for different charges and the recoil of the gun could be controlled to a better degree.

Finally, the mountain artillery: the Union mountain batteries were armed with a light 12-pounder howitzer of 4.62-inch caliber. The entire gun was only 37.2 inches long and weighed 220 pounds, and it fired an 11.5-pound spherical case shot to a range of about 1000 yards, which was generally sufficient in the tactical applications to which mountain artillery was put. The particular point about the mountain howitzer was that it could be very rapidly dismantled and loaded, in pieces, on to the back of mules. A six-gun mountain battery needed 33 mules to carry the guns and ammunition; the officers and men walked alongside.

Right: A Union 32-pounder gun on a railroad car, used outside Petersburg, Virginia.

Below: What must be the earliest armored train, this was built to provide protection for construction and repair crews rebuilding burned bridges on the Philadelphia, Wilmington & Baltimore railroad.

Railroad Artillery

The Civil War is well known for being the first war really to harness railroads to tactical and strategic maneuver, and for the reliance on railroads for supply and logistics. It comes as no surprise, therefore, to find that the idea of mounting artillery on railroad cars was soon being examined. As we have noted above, the ruling factor in the mobility of artillery was the number of horses needed to haul the gun, and this was compounded by the difficulty of hauling

Above: A 13-inch mortar on railroad flatcar preparing to bombard Richmond. Note the ammunition car and the attendant locomotive, ready to push the mortar car back into position after firing.

guns across rough country to reach specific sites from which their fire would be advantageous. There were obviously cases where existing railroad track ran in a convenient area, and even where the existing track did not go exactly where it was wanted, it was easier and quicker to set a detail of men on to laying a short spur line than it would be to clear a way and haul a heavy weapon by horse team – particularly in bad weather.

Two types of Union railroad artillery are known to have been used, notably outside Richmond. One was the standard 13-inch siege mortar mounted on a small four-wheeled flatcar; the other was a 32-pounder smooth-bore cannon, on its normal garrison wooden carriage and slide, bolted down to the bed of a specially prepared flatcar. This had ten sets of wheels to support the weight and also the shock of firing, and it was solidly protected by a massive wood and iron shield built up around the muzzle of the gun so as to give cover to the crew. The gun and carriage recoiled on the slide, so that the muzzle was inside the shield for loading, and, in general, service of the gun must have been very much the same as firing a coast defense cannon from a casemate. Just how many railroad guns were built has never been satisfactorily resolved, but the success of the guns used at Richmond must have spurred other commanders to construct similar equipment where it could conveniently be used.

Rockets

Two types of rocket were in limited use during the Civil War, though neither had much effect. The Union adopted Hale's War Rocket, an American invention, while the Confederates made one or two attempts to use Congreve's rockets, obtained from England.

Congreve's rocket was the older of the two, and the more primitive. It was simply a metal case, filled with gunpowder, attached to a stick about eight feet long, and with a small explosive shell as its warhead. The stick and rocket were laid in a long trough supported on trestles, the rocket was ignited and off it went just like a Fourth of July rocket. The shell carried a separate fuze which was lit immediately before igniting the rocket, and if the rocket gunner got his calculations right the fuze would burst the shell just as the rocket arrived at the target. Rockets of this type had been used in the United States by the British during the war of 1812, notably to set fire to parts of Washington.

Above: 'Dictator,' a celebrated 13-inch mortar used by Union troops at Richmond. Usually on a railroad car, it was here removed to a substantial ground platform for firing.

Their use by the Confederates was not attended by any considerable success. The trouble with these devices was that if the rocket was still burning when it reached the target and struck the ground, it would ricochet in whatever direction the graze had deflected it, not infrequently turning back and heading toward the launchers. It appears to have been used once or twice, under the direction of an English expert imported with the rockets, but since the result was apparently not worth the cost or trouble, the Congreve rocket was quietly abandoned.

The Hale rocket was a much more modern idea, a short tubular casing carrying a powder-filled head, and stabilized in flight by spinning. The rear of the rocket casing carried three vents, outside which were three vanes which directed the blast of the rocket slightly to one side, so causing it to spin as well as move forward. The rocket was loaded into a simple tube set on a stand and ignited. The range varied with the size of rocket, since it depended upon the amount of thrust developed by the gunpowder motor; the 2.25-inch model could reach to a mile, while the 3.25-inch model could reach about half as far again. They were more accurate than the Congreve rocket, though they still had a habit of ricocheting in various directions after impact. Their worst flaw was that faulty filling of the motor, or faulty storage, could cause the compressed gunpowder to crack or separate from the inside of the motor casing. If this happened the ignition flame would pass through or around the motor and ignite the whole lot, rather than burning on the rear surface of the motor. Ignition of the entire motor at once meant explosion, and destruction of the rocket shortly after it was launched. Although the Hale rocket was taken into service, experience soon showed that it was unreliable and, like the Congreve, it fell into disuse.

Right: Winan's Steam Gun, a somewhat impractical device intended to discharge shot by steam pressure. Captured from the Confederates in May 1861, it played no further part in the war.

Ammunition

There is little which needs to be said about the standard ammunition for smooth-bore guns. It consisted simply of a round iron ball of the correct diameter, and a charge of gunpowder contained in a cloth bag. Firing was performed by the friction primer, although a supply of loose fine powder and a linstock – a rod carrying a length of slow-burning match – were usually kept in each battery for emergency employment. The weight of the charge varied: at different times it had been

Below: A contemporary engraving of a Union 13-inch mortar which exaggerates the size in the cause of propaganda.

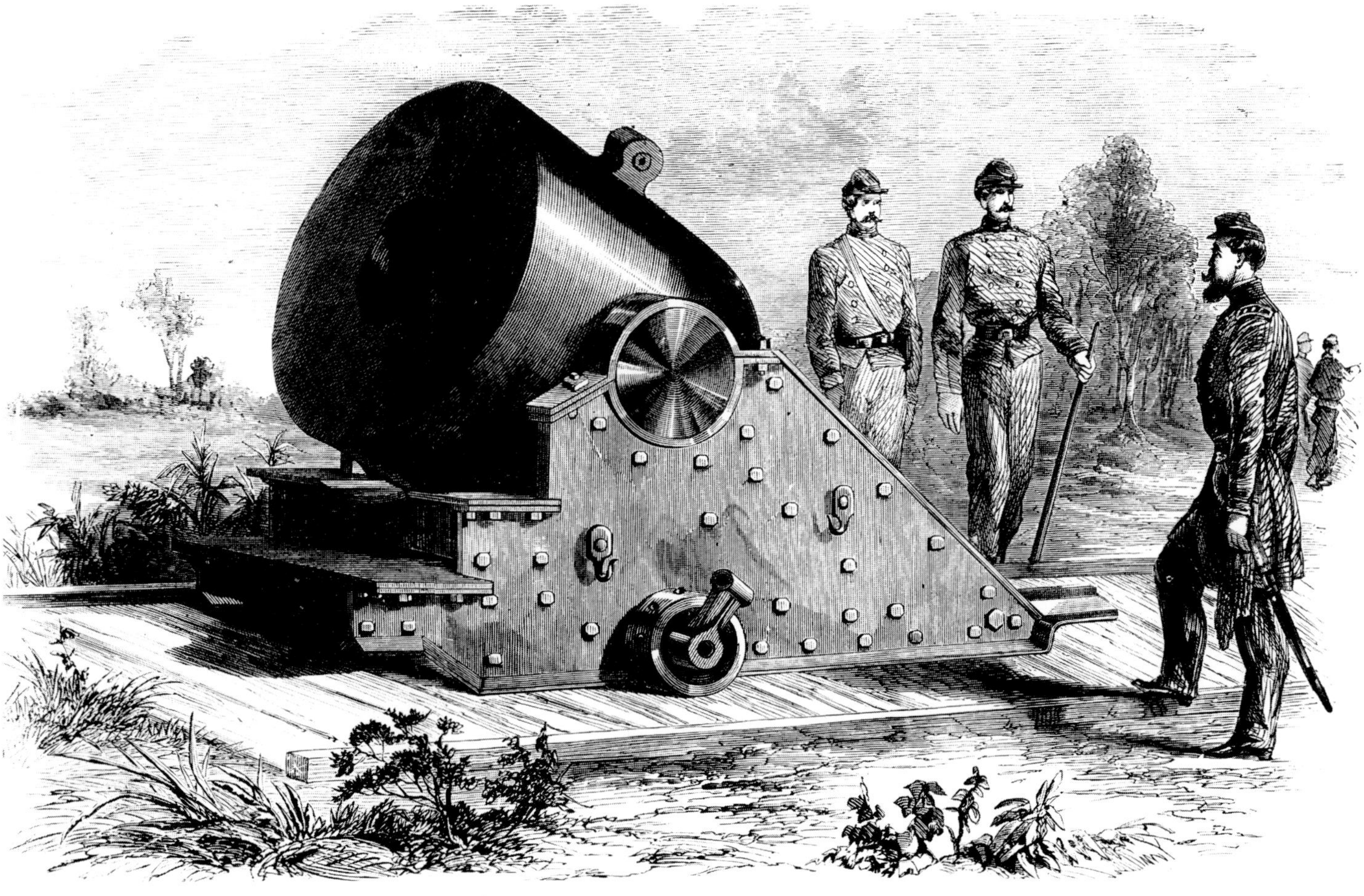

Above: A battery of 24-pounder Coehorn mortars which fired a useful 17-pound shell to a range of 1200 yards.

laid down as one-eighth, one-sixth or some other proportion of the weight of the shot. But this was really a hangover from the days of loose powder and a rule of thumb which gunners could easily remember. With the adoption of prepared cartridges, the exact amount of powder calculated to produce the best velocity and accuracy could be determined by trial firings and the arsenals would adopt this when manufacturing cartridges.

The second projectile used with smooth-bore guns was known in American service as 'Spherical Case Shot', though it was more generally known by the name of its inventor, Henry Shrapnel, as shrapnel shell. Shrapnel's object, when he first designed this projectile during the Siege of Gibraltar in the 1790s, was to deliver the equivalent of musket fire at long range. He began by taking a hollow cannon ball, filling it with a mixture of gunpowder and musket balls, and fitting it with a simple time fuze. When the time fuze burned through, it ignited the powder inside the shell, so blowing it open, and distributed the musket balls in all directions. Unfortunately, gunpowder is sensitive to friction, and several accidents occurred when the gun was fired, two or three of the musket balls nipping grains of gunpowder between them due to the shock of discharge. This was enough to fire the contents of the shell before it even got out of the gun.

Shrapnel then improved his invention by placing the musket balls in the shell, anchoring them with resin, and leaving a central hole. Into this went a tin tube filled with gunpowder, and on top of this went the fuze. Now the powder was isolated from the musket balls, and accidents became a thing of the past. It must be emphasized that the significant feature of the Shrapnel shell was that the amount of gunpowder used was the minimum which would guarantee breaking open the shell. There was no intention to give any violent impulse to the musket balls; they were endowed with the forward velocity of the shell at the moment it burst, so that they carried on the same trajectory, with the least possible disturbance from the explosion of the powder. The only drawback was that when the shell burst a proportion of the balls was directed sideways or upwards, and only some of the balls actually struck the target. This was due as much as anything to the fact that, because of its shape, there was no control over the attitude the shell might be in at the instant of bursting. In later years, when a shrapnel shell for rifled guns was perfected, the delivery of the balls became very precise and there was little or no wastage; but that was not to happen until several years after the Civil War.

Shrapnel – or spherical case – was a formidable man-killer since, exactly as its inventor had intended, it reproduced the effects of intense musket fire at ranges well beyond the power of any musket. It was the only way of delivering anti-personnel effect at long range, since explosive shells for smooth-bores were uncommon. The solid ball was, of course, a highly lethal object in its own right, but except in rare circumstances it could scarcely kill more than one or two men; a spherical case, on the other hand, could well dispose of a dozen men with a single shot.

It was possible to cut the fuze short and fire shrapnel so that it burst a short distance away from the muzzle, so producing a screen of bullets for close-in defense of the gun battery. But for this purpose the third type of projectile, the canister shot, was provided. This was no more than a thin tinplate cylinder filled with musket balls and with a heavy baseplate. When fired, it split in the bore due to the sudden acceleration, and the base plate swept everything before it, to eject a shower of balls and tinplate fragments from the gun muzzle, rather in the manner of a giant shotgun. This was deadly at close ranges, up to about 150-200 yards, and the ideal method of keeping an infantry or cavalry charge at bay.

For similar results at longer ranges, say up to 400 yards or so, the grape shot was still favored. This was a variant of canister, a solid wooden base to which a canvas bag was attached. This was filled with large 'sand shot', lead balls about one inch in diameter, and the bag was then wrapped tightly with twine. The resulting shape, with the twine pulled tightly between the sand shot, resembled a bunch of grapes, the origin of the name. When fired, it performed like canister, being ejected from the muzzle as a shower of shot, but the greater weight of the sand shot enabled them to carry further and have an effect at longer range. The only drawback was that since the sand shot were bigger, the loading of grape shot held fewer missiles. A 12-pounder canister would hold two or three hundred balls; the same size of grapeshot might hold twenty or twenty-five shot. The course of the war saw grapeshot completely displaced, since experience showed that canister at short ranges and spherical case at longer ranges gave the optimum results, rendering the carriage of a third kind of close defense projectile superfluous.

Howitzers and mortars fired shells: these were still the same spherical projectiles, but were hollow and contained a charge of gunpowder. Ideally this would be enclosed in a flannel bag, so that friction with the rough interior of the shell would not ignite the powder on discharge from the gun, but on occasion the shell was simply filled with powder and the gunners hoped for the best. The powder was ignited by a time fuze. This was no more than a round wooden peg which was drilled down the center and filled with a mixture of fine gunpowder and spirits of wine. It made a paste which held its place inside the drilled hole, and it also made a consistent filling which could be relied upon to burn at a fairly regular rate. The outside of the peg was marked off with incised lines at regular spacing, each representing an interval of time, usually one or two seconds. The gunner merely decided upon the amount of time the shell would take to reach the target – a figure which was determined by firing trials and committed to a table usually pasted inside the ammunition limber – and then, with a sharp knife

Below: The Union besiegers of Vicksburg, December 1862. A loopholed timber palisade protects both artillery and riflemen, while a sheltered dug-out serves to protect resting troops.

Above: Mound Battery, Fort Fisher, under bombardment from Admiral Porter's fleet, 15 January 1865. It was followed by a landing party which captured the fort.

or a special cutter, cut the wooden fuze at the requisite interval marker. He then drove the fuze into the hole in the shell and tore off the plaster cover over the top. This exposed a recess in the head which was filled with the gunpowder paste. The gun was then loaded, the shell being placed so that the fuze pointed toward the gun muzzle. Its position was ensured by each shell having a wooden bottom held to it by iron wires or bands; this acted as a wad between the shell and the powder charge and guaranteed that the fuze would be in the right place.

On firing the charge, a proportion of the flash of the explosion would pass over the shell in the bore and ignite the powder exposed at the head of the fuze. As the shell flew through the air the column of powder inside the wooden fuze would burn and, if the gunner had got it right, just as the shell arrived at the target the fuze would burn through and ignite the powder inside the shell, causing it to explode and throw fragments of iron in all directions.

There were occasions when the effect required was not an explosion, and here there were three special projectiles available. The first was the 'carcass', an old name for a projectile which used an iron framework but was encased in cloth or leather. It was filled with an evil mixture of turpentine, tar, resin and other combustibles, and was ignited by a fuze as it was fired. This smashed down into the enemy position and burst open, showering burning composition in all directions. The 'carcass mixture' (sometimes called 'Greek Fire') was difficult to extinguish and stuck to any surface on which it landed, to give a very good incendiary effect.

The second was the 'smoke ball', similar in construction to the carcass but filled with a composition which simply emitted a thick and choking smoke. This was used to irritate the enemy or to conceal one's own operations.

Finally, for operations at night, there was the 'light ball', another form of carcass filled with a composition containing magnesium to give a bright flame on impact. This was used to light up an enemy's position to give some indication of what he might be up to in the dark. It was also useful for firing beyond an enemy so as to silhouette his troops and defenses.

Ammunition for rifled guns opened up several new possibilities, because the elongated projectiles allowed much greater payloads to be carried, and solid shot, being heavier, had far more kinetic energy with which to smash through their targets. But the major problem here was how to load at the muzzle and yet pick up spin on the way out.

Above: A contemporary photograph showing a battery of Union artillery going into action on the south bank of the Rappahannock River, 4 June 1863. The various duties of the gunners can be easily distinguished.

We have already mentioned some of the simpler systems in passing. The basic method was to use studded and ribbed shells which engaged with the deep rifling, but this was somewhat primitive and there were plenty of inventors around who thought they could do better. As a result, the Civil War probably produced more designs for rifled-gun projectiles than any other comparable period of time.

The next most obvious solution was to use the gas pressure in the exploding charge to make some change in the shell's outline so that it would grip the rifling. Among the more simple of these ideas was the Parrott shell, which had a saucer-shaped disc of brass attached to the base. Due to the bend of the saucer, the edge of the disc was slightly below the edge of the shell when it was loaded, so that the shell slipped into the bore quite easily, but the pressure of the explosion flattened out the saucer so that its rim expanded beyond the diameter of the shell and engaged in the rifling grooves. The Parrott-Reed shell was similar in principle, using a copper or wrought-iron ring and varying the method of attachment to the shell. The method of attachment was, of course, somewhat critical, since it had to be able to transmit the torque, induced into the cup by the rifling, to the shell so that it spun. The Parrott and Parrott-Reed shells were probably the most successful of all these designs, though they tended to cast their driving plates during flight, which could be dangerous for any friendly troops underneath the trajectory. In any event, the Union Army acquired well over a million of these shells in various calibers.

The Confederate Army adopted a similar system, using a copper or soft iron plate; the interesting part about this design was the attachment, using a central bolt screwed into the shell base, together with three pins cast into the plate which engaged with three holes in the shell. The central bolt took care of attachment, while the three pins acted as the torque drivers.

The Schenkl shell was of iron and carried a long tapering tail cast with longitudinal ribs. Around the rear of this tail was a papier-mâché cylinder, set in place around the ribs. On firing, the gas pressure drove the papier-mâché forward, compressing it and, due to the taper on the shell tail, forcing it out to engage with the rifling. Spin was transferred to the shell by the ribs on the tail, and the force of ejecting the projectile usually split the papier-mâché cylinder so that once it left the muzzle it fell away from the shell. The only defect with this idea was that the quality of the papier-mâché was variable; when it was well

Above: A Confederate battery at Vicksburg. Note the waterproof covers placed over the firing vents of the guns, an indication that they are loaded and ready for immediate action.

made and varnished to protect it from damp all was well, but if the quality was poor or the varnishing badly done so that the cylinder swelled, loading could be difficult, if not impossible. And if the cylinder broke up in the bore, the shell would be unstable and inaccurate in flight.

Again, the Confederates used a very similar idea, though in their case instead of the papier-mâché cylinder they employed a simple lead or copper ring around the projectile tail. Gas pressure blew this forward, and the taper expanded it into the grooves. We have very little hard information on the use of this method, but it would appear to be better than the Union design.

Benjamin Berkeley Hotchkiss, who later gave his name to the Hotchkiss machine gun, was, by the time of the Civil War, a man of some experience in firearms manufacture and design, and he spread his net a little further during the war to cover artillery. He developed another expanding shell which was manufactured in large numbers for the Union forces. It was in two parts, the fore part having a rounded nose and then a body tapering to a short stem, and the rear section cylindrical and fitted around the stem of the fore part, leaving a gap at the side of the shell. This was filled with lead, and when the shell was fired the gas pressure thrust the rear section tight against the fore part, thus squeezing the lead outward to bite into the rifling. The squeezed lead tended to develop a ragged edge which was flung outward by centrifugal force during the shell's flight and often gave rise to odd noises; these were thought by the Union troops to add to the attraction of the shell, striking fear into the enemy. In fact, knowing what we now know about ballistics and the flight of shells, such 'fringeing' was probably costing the shell ten percent of its range and ruining the accuracy into the bargain.

The 'James Conversion' was mentioned earlier, a system of cutting rifling into old smoothbores in order to bring them up to date; these guns were accompanied by a shell, also designed by James, which again relied upon gas pressure for its functioning. The shell body was egg-shaped, with a cast-iron skirt around the rear end. This skirt was slotted, the slots were filled with lead and the exterior covered with a thin layer of tin. On firing the gas pressure entered the interior of the skirt and, passing through the slots, forced the lead out into the rifling, deforming the tin as it did so. Since the lead remained partly in the slots and partly in the rifling, it transferred the torque to the shell. It was a complicated system of manufacture, but several thousand were made for the Union Army. It went out of use before the war

Above: A contemporary engraving entitled 'A Battery before Petersburg.' Of interest is the mantlet of woven rope hung across the gun embrasure to stop bullets and splinters from striking the men operating the gun.

Below: Union artillery at drill, Fort Totten, New York. The guns are 24-pounders on garrison carriages, for the defense of forts and harbors.

ended, simply because the James guns failed to last the course.

The Archer shell was a Confederate invention, similar in concept to the Hotchkiss shell in that it came in two parts and had a lead driving band in between them. In this case the rear section was a wooden ring, and both it and the lead band were covered in a sheet of tin. This had the virtue of holding everything together, even if it did little for the mechanical action of engraving in the rifling.

One projectile no reference work on the Civil War fails to mention is the 'Confederate Winged Shot', though nobody seems very sure who invented it or where it was used. One such example exists in a museum collection, but there is no guarantee that it represents a projectile actually approved for service. The shot takes the form of an ovoid head with a short tail stem, ending in a caliber-width cup. Alongside the narrow stem are two spring-loaded fins which lie within the caliber while loaded and then spring out as the shot leaves the muzzle of the gun. The cup-shaped rear portion would expand under gas pressure and so seal the bore, while the fins were presumably intended to bestow some degree of stabilization in flight. They might have done, but their effect would be minimal, and it is very doubtful if this projectile ever worked as its inventor hoped.

Fuzes

With the growing number of hollow gunpowder-filled shells that were coming into use, it became necessary to develop suitable fuzes. The fuze previously described, the old wooden peg which was cut off at the appropriate length and inserted into a spherical shell, was adequate for its day, but by the 1860s its day was long past, and something more accurate was wanted. Moreover, with the advent of rifled guns with shells which sealed the bore very effectively, the old style of ignition, relying upon the propellant flash to wash over the shell and ignite the fuze, was no longer reliable.

With the use of rifled guns, it was now possible to foretell which end of the shell was going to hit the target first, and this led to the increasing employment of impact fuzes. In cannon-ball days, when the shell was rolling over and over as it flew, there was no hope of knowing how the shell would land, and the only way to obtain an impact burst was to devise some sort of fuze which would function irrespective of the shell's attitude. This was not impossible, but the solutions which had been arrived at were invariably extremely sensitive and unsafe.

The first improvement in time fuzes came with the adoption of a set of standardized units. The gunner was provided with a quantity of wooden pegs bored with a central hole, which could be driven into the fuze-hole in the shell. He was then supplied with boxes of paper fuzes, short tubes filled with carefully made cores of fuze powder which, due to their composition and dimensions, burned for a specified time. The different times were colour-coded: black fuzes burned an inch in two seconds, red an inch in three seconds and so on. Deciding upon the time required; the gunner would select a fuze of the correct type; if the time demanded a fraction of a second, he would clip off part of the paper tube. Having made his selection, he simply pushed the tube into the central core of the wooden peg, loaded the shell and fired it. Ignition was by flash-over, in the accepted manner.

The second improvement came with the Borman fuze, a self-contained, pre-timed unit which the gunner merely had to cut and fix into the shell. The Borman fuze was of metal, a screwed shank with a circular cap carrying time markings from zero to 5.5 seconds. Inside the cap was a ring of powder composition, covered with a thin layer of metal, and the paper carrying the time markings. One end of the powder ring connected to an internal passage leading to a charge of gunpowder held in the threaded portion of the fuze. All that was necessary was for the gunner to screw the fuze into the head of the shell and then, with an awl, a knife or some other instrument, punch a hole in the top corresponding to whatever time he desired. On firing the flashover would light the train of powder at the point exposed by the punched hole; the train would then burn round the

Right: Palmetto Battery of the Confederate artillery, at Charleston SC in 1863. The guns appear to be light 12-pounders, Model of 1841.

Right: Examples of projectiles for the Whitworth rifled gun, which used a twisted hexagonal bore and had the projectiles shaped to suit.

fuze, eventually arriving at the passage and igniting the gunpowder at the correct time interval. The gunpowder would blow out through the bottom of the fuze and so ignite the contents of the shell. The accuracy attained with this fuze made it ideal for use with spherical case shot, which, to be most effective, needed to be burst some fifty yards in front of the enemy.

The rifled Armstrong gun, because of its tight-fitting lead-coated shell, required a fuze which did not rely on flash-over for ignition, and Armstrong provided one, known as the 'Armstrong E Fuze' since it was his fifth attempt before he got the design to work properly. It was of metal, brass or an alloy, and came in three parts. The base of the fuze, which screwed into the head of the shell, carried a part-circular ring of fine gunpowder and, in its center, a percussion cap held above a fixed firing pin by a spring. There was a short passage between the chamber holding this cap and the end of the gunpowder train. In the center of the base, above the cap chamber, was a central stem, threaded at its top and with a deep groove cut into its circumference just below the thread. Cut into the side of this stem was a vertical groove which connected with the circular groove and carried a length of gunpowder-soaked thread which led down into the bottom of the fuze where there was a charge of gunpowder.

Around this central stem fitted the second part, a ring of metal with, at one point, an upstanding lug engraved with a vertical line. Inside this lug was a chamber, filled with gunpowder, and a port leading to the inside surface of the ring and aligned with the groove running around the central stem. Finally, this ring was held tight to the body of the fuze by a screw cap on top of the stem.

To set the fuze the gunner loosened the screw cap and rotated the ring until the vertical index mark was opposite the selected time, engraved on a scale around the body of the fuze. He then tightened up the cap securely, screwed the fuze into the shell, loaded and fired. On firing the sudden shock caused the percussion cap to overcome its spring and hit the fixed firing pin beneath; the flash shot through the port and lit the gunpowder train. This burned around the ring until it met the chamber full of gunpowder in the movable ring, whereupon this gunpowder was ignited; it flashed through to the groove around the central stem and ignited the quick-match, which then ignited the gunpowder in the base of the fuze, which in turn blew out and fired the contents of the shell. The Armstrong E Fuze was very reliable, and remained in British Army service until the 1890s.

Impact fuzes could be of two sorts: in modern terminology they were either direct action or graze, although these terms were not used in the 1860s. The direct action type relied upon the impact to drive a cap against a fixed firing pin; in the graze pattern, on the other hand, the firing pin was held firmly in front of a loose metal pellet carrying the cap and allowed the sudden stopping of the shell to throw the pellet forward and so impale the cap on the firing pin. The advantage of

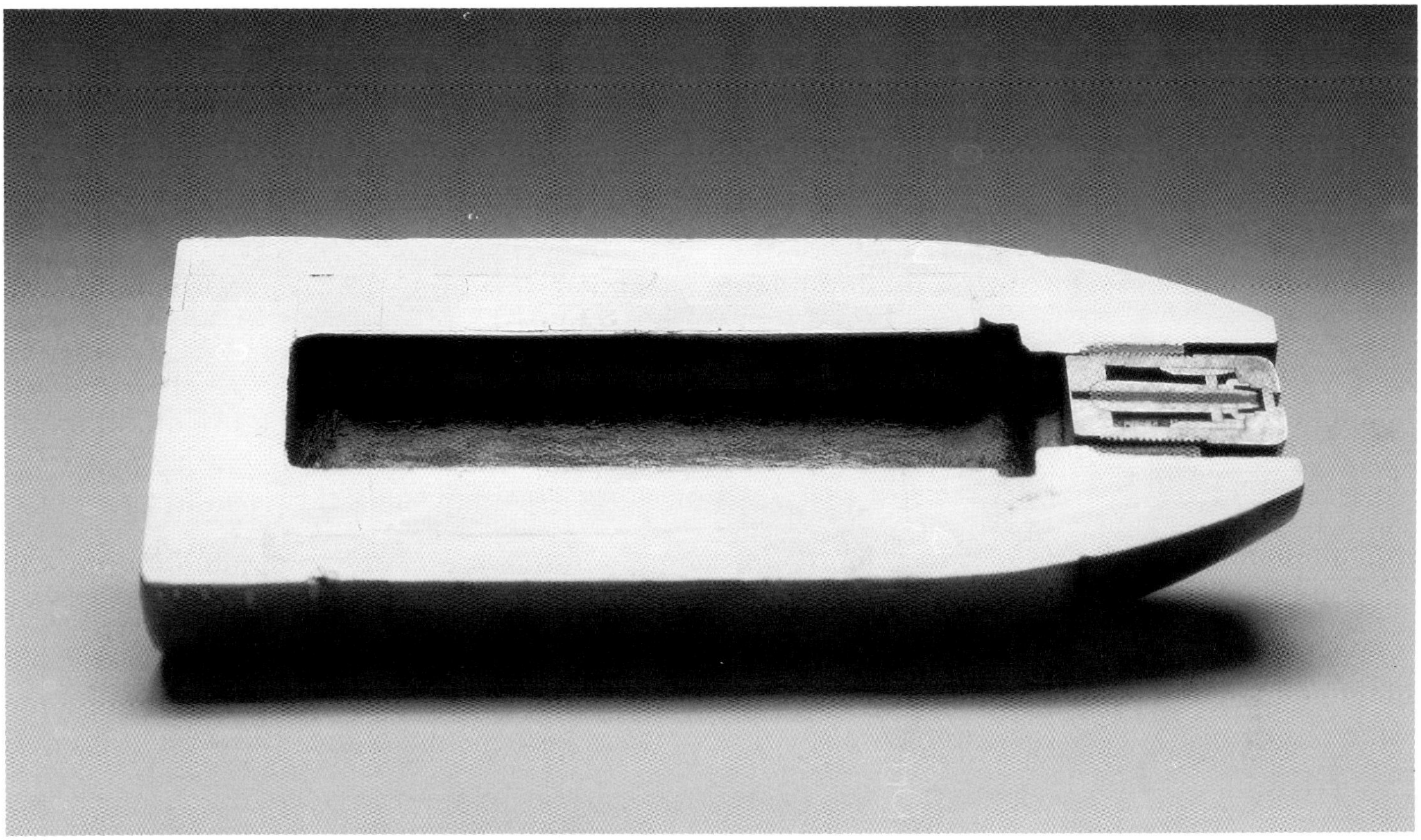

Above: A 25-pounder Armstrong shell, cut open to reveal the relatively small space for powder, and fitted with a concussion fuze.

the latter type was that if the shell landed obliquely, so that only its shoulder struck the target, the sudden check to its progress would be sufficient to set the pellet forward and fire the shell. The direct action fuze, on the other hand, demanded a square impact on its head in order to drive in the cap and explode the charge in the shell.

As an example of the direct action pattern, a common type was simply a hollow brass bolt with the central tube closed at the rear end by a wooden or cork plug. The tube was then filled with gunpowder and closed at the front by a screwed metal plug having a hollow firing pin in the center. Above this was a metal cover holding a simple percussion cap in its center. As the shell struck, so the cover was driven in, the cap hit the firing pin, the flash went through the hollow pin to ignite the gunpowder inside the fuze, and the subsequent explosion blew out the rear plug and ignited the contents of the shell.

The graze fuze is perhaps best exemplified by the design produced by Hotchkiss; of all the Civil War designs this was the only one which achieved any lasting fame, being widely used throughout the world in improved forms well into the twentieth century. It consisted of a brass tube, partially screw-threaded, enclosed at its front end by a cap with a fixed firing pin pointing back into the center of the fuze. Inside the fuze was a lead pellet carrying a percussion cap; this had two pieces of wire attached, which were led out through a hole in the bottom of the fuze. This hole was tapered inward to the fuze interior, and the wires were trapped in place by a lead plug driven into this tapered hole. The positioning of the wires was such that the pellet inside the fuze was held well away from the firing pin, and it could not move in any direction because of the wires.

On firing, the sudden acceleration of the shell under the impulse of the propelling charge caused the lead pellet holding the wires to fall free into the interior of the shell. This same 'set-back' force also drove the interior pellet to the bottom of the fuze, where it stayed during the flight of the shell. In fact, due to the gradual deceleration of the shell during flight because of air resistance and gravity, this pellet would begin to creep forward very slightly, but not with sufficient speed to have any effect. Once the shell struck the target, the pellet was flung forward with such force that the cap was fired by the pin, and the flash passed through a hole in the center of the pellet, through the hole in the bottom of the fuze, and ignited the shell's contents.

Similar fuzes were made by Parrott, Schenkl and Absterdam, all of which used some shearable device to hold the inertia pellet safe until the gun was fired. Parrott used two pins which were broken on set-back, Schenkl a thin screw inserted through the side of the fuze, which likewise broke on firing, and the Absterdam fuze used a lead sleeve into which the pellet set back. None of these proved as reliable as the Hotchkiss design, which is why they failed to survive the war years.

4

THE NAVAL WAR

Previous page: The first clash between ironclad warships: the CSS *Virginia* and the USS *Monitor* exchange shots in Hampton Roads, 9 March 1862.

Right: A gun crew on the Union gunboat *Thomas Freeborn*, credited with firing the US Navy's first offensive shot in the Civil War on 29 May 1861 against a Confederate shore battery.

Apart from a few well-known incidents, the naval side of the Civil War is less known and understood than the land campaigns; yet many commentators aver that the naval operations of the Union were far more vital to the overall strategy of the war than most of the land operations. Early in the war General Winfield Scott had propounded the 'Anaconda Plan', less of a plan than an outline idea. A shrewd soldier, he could see, when others preferred not to think about it, that the war was not going to be won within the enlistment period of the first 90-day volunteers. It was going to be a long war, and the way it should be fought, according to Scott, was to envelop and strangle the Confederacy. The US Navy should blockade the coasts; the Army should then advance down the Mississippi River until it reached the Gulf of Mexico, laying down a barrier which would split the Confederacy away from the western states. The Mississippi valley would then be held in strength, and since nothing could then reach the South either from the west overland or from the east by sea, the insurrection would be isolated. With this done, the Army could then maneuver at leisure and crush the Confederates piece by piece.

Scott's theories were scoffed at by most people and derided in the newspapers, but he had the ear of President Lincoln, and, diluted in some respects, his plan became the basic Union strategy. Shortly after the attack on Fort Sumter, Lincoln proclaimed a blockade of the Southern states. This was all very fine, except that the Union simply had very little with which to carry out such a blockade, and before long they had even less. The Confederates made a raid on Norfolk, Virginia and in the face of the approaching attack the staff at Norfolk set fire to everything burnable and decamped, with the result that 10 warships and most of the naval stores were destroyed. What was even worse was that several hundred

Below: A Union river gunboat, designed in the same manner as the CSS *Virginia*, using a timber wall supported by iron framing to protect the gun battery and pilot house.

Above: Admiral Porter's fleet running the Mississippi blockade at Vicksburg, 16 April 1863.

cannon were stored in Norfolk Navy Yard and, these being indestructible by fire, the Confederates got the lot. So not only had the Union lost a naval base, it had lost a good deal of its navy and most of its reserve of equipment.

Gideon Welles, Secretary of the Navy, and Gustavus Fox, his Assistant Secretary, were probably two of the best administrators Lincoln had, and they set to work to build up the Union Navy from virtually nothing. Every seaport in Union territory was combed for all the available vessels which could, by any shift or expedient, be made to serve, and these were bought, chartered or commandeered. The government yards were immediately ordered to begin construction of eight sloops of war, while private yards were told to produce 23 screw gunboats as fast as possible.

The standard warships of the period were still of wooden construction, with masts and yards for a spread of sail, but by this time the steam engine had become a practical machine and screw or paddle propulsion was provided. Though not the principal method of moving the ship – sails were still provided for use whenever the wind was available – it was a system which could be employed when there was insufficient wind or when maneuvering in confined waters.

But as fate would have it the commencement of the Civil War came at a time when the warship was undergoing perhaps its most important revolution. In 1858 the French had begun building *La Gloire*, the world's first ironclad warship, and in 1859, by way of response, the British had laid down the *Warrior*, not only ironclad but built entirely of iron. Moreover, it had been only a few years since the French Navy had operated 'floating batteries', protected by iron armor, against the Russian forts in the Crimea. As a result, by 1861 the idea of armor protection for warships was being studied by naval authorities all over the world, and among them was the Confederate Navy.

The Confederate Navy had been non-existent, of course, prior to the outbreak of war, and it had to be built up from nothing. Like the Union, the Confederates had the good fortune to find a Secretary of the Navy who was competent and active. Stephen Mallory scoured his seaports for useful ships, made arrangements to buy from abroad where possible, and above all searched the Southern states for iron and steel with which to construct his own fleet of ironclads. He had no hope of competing with the Union on quantity, so he decided to do what he could to defeat them by technical superiority. Factories had to be found and equipped to manufacture boilers and engines, armament for the ships had to be found or made (the loot from Norfolk Navy Yard partially solved this problem), and, most difficult of all, he had to find officers and crews to man the ships.

There was no shortage of recruits; the only trouble was that few of them had ever even smelt the sea, let alone sailed on it.

While the two sides were thus attempting to get their naval strength organized, the blockade was already taking shape. In August 1861 an expedition was mounted by General Butler which captured two Confederate forts at Hatteras Inlet. A small garrison, with a flotilla of light craft, was left to seal up this doorway to the South, while the rest of the force went back to Hampton Roads. The Navy now decided that it would be wise to seize a suitable base for operations further down the coast, and argued for a similar expedition to capture Port Royal, South Carolina. Unfortunately General McClellan failed to see the point of this and refused troops. Hardly had he done so when General Burnside appeared and suggested an expedition to the Hatteras Inlet once more, this time to sail in, upriver, and destroy whatever Confederate installations he could find. For some reason or other McClellan decided this was feasible and gave Burnside his blessing. Then General Butler sprang to life and sailed from Hampton Roads once more, this time to capture and garrison Ship Island, in the Gulf of Mexico, close to the entrance to Mobile Bay. So by the end of 1861 the Union had a thin but effective cordon around the Southern seaboard.

The naval war got underway in the spring of 1862 when Admiral Porter took a Union fleet down to Ship Island and began to make preparations to attack New Orleans. The entrance to the Mississippi was guarded by two powerful forts flanking the river, and it was the accepted rule of the day that ships were powerless against forts. Porter disagreed. He assembled a fleet of barges, mounted 13-inch mortars on them, had them towed up to suitable locations and then set about a terrible bombardment of the two forts. While this was taking place a second fleet, under Admiral Farragut, ran between the forts, defying Confederate fire-ships and gunboats, as well as the fire from those guns which had not yet suffered from Porter's attentions. The operation was a complete success, New Orleans was captured and most of the Mississippi River was now in Union hands.

McClellan now moved down from Washington with his army, intending to take Richmond; daunted by the defenses, and tricked by the Confederate General Magruder into thinking that Richmond was more strongly defended than it actually was, McClellan was stalled. The obvious answer, so far as he saw it, was to take to the water again and outflank the Richmond position. But now the Confederates played a new card. They unveiled their first ironclad.

Below: The CSS *Virginia* sinking the USS *Cumberland* by ramming in Hampton Roads, 8 March 1862.

When the Confederates raided Norfolk, one of the things they salvaged was the USS *Merrimac*, or what was left of her. A frigate, she had been set on fire and had burned to the waterline and foundered, but the Confederates raised the wreck and found what was left still sound. On top of the hull they built a fresh upperworks composed of sloping timbers sheathed in two two-inch layers of iron – rolled from railroad track – and behind this they placed heavy guns. Two seven-inch rifled guns were placed on pivots at bow and stern; a 6.4-inch rifled gun and three nine-inch smooth-bores were mounted on each broadside. Driven by steam, the CSS *Virginia*, as she now was, could make five knots through the water, and was furnished with an iron ram on her bows.The weight of this enormous casemate caused the hull to settle down in the water until the bow and stern were almost invisible, with the result that from a distance it looked as if some odd building was floating across the sea.

On 8th March 1862 the CSS *Virginia* sailed into Hampton Roads in search of something to destroy. Her first target was the USS *Cumberland*, toward which she confidently sailed. The *Cumberland*'s captain took one look as this floating monstrosity, called his crew to arms and opened fire, only to watch in dismay as the shot bounced off the sloping pent roof of the strange vessel 'like hailstones off a tin roof'. The captain of the *Virginia*, for his part, saw that the enemy could do him little harm and forebore to fire; he merely sailed serenely on and despatched the *Cumberland* with his iron ram. Having done this, the *Virginia* turned about and set off after the USS *Congress*, against which she opened fire with explosive shells, soon reducing her to a smoking shambles. A third Union warship managed to run aground in attempting to escape, and the *Virginia* sailed back to her berth well satisfied with the day's work. But, by a most remarkable coincidence, as the *Virginia* sailed home, into the other end of the Roads came the Union response: the ironclad *Monitor*.

The Union Navy had received information about the building of the *Virginia* almost as soon as it had been planned, and, seeking to fight fire with fire, they canvassed for something similar, a 'steam ironclad floating battery'. In reply came John Ericsson, seeking to expound his theories.

Ericsson had been born in Sweden in 1803; in 1820 he became an engineer in the Swedish Army, and in 1826 went to England to learn about steam engines, later being involved in the construction of some of the earliest locomotives. In 1836 he had invented a screw propeller for ships, and offered this to the British Admiralty. They were unreceptive, and Ericsson therefore took himself off to America, remaining there until his death in 1889.

In the early 1850s he had designed an armored floating battery with a revolving gun turret; this had been offered to the French Navy, who turned it down. In late 1861 he appeared in Washington

Below: The USS *Cumberland*, damaged by ramming and under fire, sinks after its attack by the CSS *Virginia*.

Right: Captain John Ericsson, inventor of the turret ship and designer of the USS *Monitor*.

and offered a similar device to the Union Navy. They were somewhat resistant, but when the news about the building of the *Virginia* reached them, Ericsson's ideas suddenly appeared most attractive, and the Navy Board gave him instructions to start building.

Ericsson's *Monitor* was a completely new type of ship, doubtless because it was designed by an engineer rather than by a shipwright. Instead of adopting the traditional type of hull, *Monitor* was simply an enormous raft 172 feet long and 41.5 feet wide, given buoyancy by a box-like hull 124 feet long and 34 feet wide. The overhanging raft construction was designed to provide the most stable gun platform possible, so as to permit the most accurate fire, and it also protected the hull from any attack by ramming, since an attacking vessel would smash its hull against the raft long before its ram could reach the recessed hull. The vessel displaced 987 tons, had a draft of 10.5 feet and was driven at a maximum speed of nine knots by two steam engines.

The raft was protected by 4.5 inches of wrought-iron plate supported by timber, and centrally on this superstructure was the turret. This circular structure was 20 feet in diameter, built of eight-inch iron plate and contained two 11-inch Dahlgren smooth-bore cannons. The entire turret could be rotated by a steam engine inside the hull which was connected to a central shaft. The turret floor carried two sets of slides upon which the gun carriages could recoil. The guns were to be manually run in for loading the first shot; during the loading, massive hinged plates called 'port-stoppers' would be swung so as to close the gunports, preventing any stray shot or splinters from entering the turret. Once the guns were loaded the stoppers were swung aside and the guns run forward by rope tackle. On firing, the recoil brought them back inside the turret, the stoppers were closed and reloading began.

Ericsson received his contract in October 1861; *Monitor* was launched in January 1862, having been built at the Continental Iron Works, Greenpoint, New York. After being armed and undergoing some short trials, in March she set sail from New York to Hampton Roads, running into a storm and almost foundering *en route*. She may have been the last word in armored floating batteries, but she was no sort of seaboat; the low freeboard allowed water to pour over the raft and enter ventilation hatches in the hull, while the action of the waves beneath the raft appeared to be separating it from the hull. And while this voyage was in progress *Virginia* appeared and began her short reign of terror in Hampton Roads. *Monitor* was being sent there merely as a routine move, it being apparently a useful location; that *Virginia* should suddenly appear was in nobody's mind, and thus the fact that the two ironclads came together so promptly is one of the great coincidences of the war.

On 9th March the two contestants moved into the ring. The word had spread rapidly around the area and the shores were thick with spectators come to see the great battle. After maneuvering around each other like a pair of heavyweights (which, in a sense, they were) they opened fire. The *Monitor*'s shots struck the *Virginia*'s iron carapace and bounced off; *Virginia*'s shots struck the iron turret or the armored raft and bounced off. *Virginia* tried to ram, but in the first place her cast-iron ram had been twisted off by her assault on *Cumberland* on the previous day, and in the second place the construction of *Monitor*, and her superior speed, rendered the maneuver impotent. More gunnery followed. The turret crew of *Monitor* found that their port-stoppers were jamming, so they left them open and, using the steam engine, turned the turret away from the enemy in order to load, then swung it back. But there was a defect in the engine controls, so that they had to fire the guns as they swung across the target. *Virginia* hit *Monitor* 22 times, nine of the shots

Right: The crew of the USS *Monitor* relax on the deck of their unusual warship after the battle. Note the dent in the turret, made by a Confederate shot.

Above: The surrender of the Confederate ironclad *Tennessee* during the Battle of Mobile Bay.

striking the turret and making slight dents. Eventually the captain of *Virginia* turned away. His gunnery officer had stopped firing and on being asked why replied: 'I could do as much damage by snapping my fingers every three minutes.' *Monitor*'s captain also turned away, since his gunners had run out of ammunition. After some three or four hours of fruitless counter-fire the battle was over, the result a draw.

The two ships never met again: each side was uneasy in case such a battle came to a conclusive end and their ship was sunk. The presence of the *Virginia* restricted Union activity in Hampton Roads, just as the presence of *Monitor* kept the Confederates at bay. Meanwhile the land battle continued, though any hopes of a seaborne flanking movement were effectively dashed by the looming presence of the *Virginia*. Eventually the

Right: The CSS *Atlanta*, one of several ironclads built after the pattern of the *Virgina* and used to patrol the major rivers.

Above: The USS *Hartford*, Admiral Farragut's flagship, attacking the Confederate ironclad *Tennessee* during the Battle of Mobile Bay.

Union troops broke through and Norfolk was recaptured. Before leaving, on 11th May 1862, the Confederates set fire to the *Virginia*, since its draft was too great to allow them to sail it upriver to safety. Once the flames reached the magazine, the ship was utterly destroyed.

Monitor also met an inelegant end. At the end of the year it was decided to return her to New York. Off Cape Hatteras, being towed in rough seas, she was swamped by waves which poured into the hull beneath the turret, and she sank on 31st December 1862 taking with her 14 of her crew of 49.

Notwithstanding that the Battle of Hampton Roads had been inconclusive, both sides now plunged into the building of ironclads as hard as they could, both for sea use (though in sheltered waters only) and for patrolling the Mississippi. Both sides stuck with what they knew and what they could manage to build; the Confederates continued with the pattern set up by *Virginia*, a slope-roofed floating battery, while the Union Navy stuck with Ericsson's revolving turret. For riverine work the screw was less favored than the paddle as a means of propulsion, since the latter gave better maneuverability in confined waters. The problem was to protect the vulnerable paddles from gunfire, and this was achieved either by building armored casings outboard of the paddles, or by designing a stern-wheel paddle ship with the paddles concealed inside the ironclad hull.

It is not often remembered that the Civil War gave birth to a particular class of warship which is still used today, though much changed in form and employment: the cruiser. In 1863 the Union Navy began building a new type of warship whose purpose was to go out on to the high seas and overtake Confederate blockade-runners. Their purpose was simply to destroy the Confederate merchant marine without being themselves drawn into battle with other warships except in favorable circumstances or when unavoidable. The first of these was the USS *Idaho*, of which history says little except that she was a failure, presumably not being fast enough. Eventually the designers got it right with the USS *Wampanoag* and her two sister ships. These could reach a speed of 17 knots and carried 16 10- or 11-inch broadside guns and a revolving 60-pounder rifle in the bows.

Naval Ordnance

All guns work on similar principles, though you would be hard put to convince a sailor of this. There is no good technical reason why land service guns should not be fired from ships; all I know is that it has rarely happened, though many naval guns have been happily adopted by land service artillery throughout the years. Sailors always know best, and they always have to have something different, and it was thus during the American Civil War.

John Augustus Dahlgren has been called 'The Father of American Naval Ordnance', with some justification. Joining the Navy in 1826, in 1847 he commanded an Ordnance Workshop in Washington Navy Yard which later became the Naval Gun Factory. In 1862 he was appointed Chief of the Bureau of Ordnance, then went to sea to command the Union's South Atlantic Blockading Squadron for the remainder of the war. He then commanded the South Pacific Squadron until 1868, when he returned for a second tour as Chief of the Bureau of Ordnance. He died, holding the rank of Rear-Admiral, in 1870.

In his workshop in Washington, in 1848, he began designing guns, his first being a small bronze howitzer for boat service. At about this time he discovered the writings of General Paixhans, a French soldier who had made several cogent suggestions for the rearmament of the French Navy. Briefly, Paixhans argued for a rational range of calibers and the adoption of shell-firing guns. Instead of having guns of half a dozen calibers on board a warship, Paixhans suggested adopting one caliber and having lighter and heavier guns, so simplifying ammunition provision and supply. And since this would scarcely be practical with shot-firing guns (for the lighter weapons would fire their shot at too low a velocity to be of use) this argued the adoption of powder-filled shells as the standard projectile. The explosive force of the shell would be sufficient to damage the enemy, and the lessened recoil and lighter charges used with the guns would lead to a faster rate of fire. His recommendations were looked at by the French Navy and they adopted the idea of a rationalized caliber in the early 1840s.

Dahlgren thought about these ideas but objected to the shell gun proposition since he felt it was too limiting; he decided that what was needed was a gun capable of firing either shell or

Below: Admiral Dahlgren, alongside a gun of his design, after the Civil War had ended.

Above: Union sailors and marines manning a Dahlgren gun on board a warship.

shot as the occasion demanded, and he advocated fitting warships completely with such guns instead of the mixture of shot and shell guns then being generally argued.

In 1850 a nine-inch gun to Dahlgren's designs was cast at the West Point Foundry. It weighed 9080 pounds with a rather angular outline. It was successfully fired on test, but Dahlgren was not satisfied and designed a fresh model, making the outline more gracefully curved and giving it two firing vents, each with a hammer lock for use with friction tubes. This was successful,

Right: Acting Master Eben M Stoddard (left) and Chief Engineer William H Cushman standing by an 11-inch Rodman gun on board the USS *Kearsarge*. Note the grapeshot on the deck in front of the gun carriage.

A somewhat embroidered depiction of the battle between the *Monitor* and the *Virginia*, with the previous day's sinking of the *Cumberland* thrown in for good measure.

Above: The interior of the turret on the USS *Monitor*, showing the two 11-inch Dahlgren guns and one of the port-stoppers closed.

and he then designed an 11-inch along the same lines; both guns were accepted as the standard US naval ordnance in the 1850s.

The Battle of Hampton Roads had been watched by Augustus Fox, the Assistant Secretary of the Union Navy, and the inconclusive end of the battle led him to the belief that 11-inch guns were not sufficient to deal with ironclads. He therefore called upon Dahlgren to design something more powerful, and in April 1862 Dahlgren responded with a 15-inch gun, specifically designed for mounting inside the Ericsson turrets on the monitors then being built. (The name of the ship had now been transformed into a general class name, and was to remain so.) This monster weighed 42,000 pounds and could fire a 440-pound solid shot by means of a 60-pound propelling charge of powder; or a 400-pound hollow shot intended for use against fortifications; or a 330-pound explosive shell containing 13 pounds of gunpowder. This latter proved highly effective in various engagements with Confederate ships during the war.

By the time the gun foundry began producing the 15-inch gun, the construction of the new class of monitors was well under way, and, of course, the turrets had been designed around the dimensions of the original *Monitor*, for two 11-inch guns. Moreover, the rate of production of 15-inch Dahlgrens was unable to catch up with that of the ships, so the earliest of the new monitors were actually armed with one 11-inch and one 15-inch gun in the turret. Another drawback was that the gun ports in the turret had been designed to permit the 11-inch gun muzzle to project through when firing, but they were too small to allow the 15-inch muzzle to pass, although they were big enough to allow the 15-inch shell to be fired through. Since firing the 15-inch inside the turret would have been intolerable for the crew, a 'smoke-box' of wrought iron was built inside the 15-inch gun port. When the gun was run forward to fire, its muzzle entered this box; on firing, the box deflected much of the smoke and blast and directed it through the gun port, keeping the noise and smoke down to a more tolerable level inside the turret.

Dahlgren was now asked to do even better and develop a 20-inch gun for adoption in the forthcoming Puritan class of monitors. He designed the gun quickly enough, but the foundry ran into problems in casting such an enormous weapon, and at the same time the Navy Board, the Bureau of Ships and Ericsson got into a long and highly involved argument about the design of the monitors. As a result none of the Puritan class was built by the time the war ended, and shortly afterward the whole idea was abandoned, and with it the

20-inch Dahlgren gun. The 15-inch Dahlgren, together with the 15-inch Rodman guns developed for the Army, were to be the high-water mark of the smooth-bore gun era.

Dahlgren ignored the rifled gun, probably because he left the post of Chief of Ordnance before he had time to give the matter much thought. His successor took the simplest way of obtaining rifled guns by turning to Parrott at the West Point Foundry and instructing him to produce guns for the Union Navy. But, true to the tradition outlined above, the guns which Parrott was producing for the Army were not considered suitable; he had to develop special designs for the Navy. The 100-pounder Army Parrott gun was 151 inches long; the Navy 100-pounder was 130 inches long, the reason given being that the confined space of a naval gun deck restricted the distance that a gun could be run in for loading, and thus the barrel had to be shorter so as to clear the gun port and leave loading room. The Army's 200-pounder Parrott was considered far too long and therefore a special 150-pounder was produced for the Navy, 136 inches long, firing a 152-pound shell. The 30-pounder Army Parrott gun weighed 4200 pounds and was 136 inches long; the Navy 30-pounder weighed 3550 pounds and was 97 inches long; and so on.

Unfortunately, the Parrott guns adopted by the Navy soon acquired a most unsavory reputation. They developed a habit of bursting. Much of this was due to the strain on the metal due to the method of construction; it will be recalled that the basic Parrott system was a cast-iron gun with a wrought-iron hoop shrunk around the breech end over the chamber so as to resist the highest pressure. But, probably under the strains of wartime production, the delicate dimensioning which this system demanded was sometimes not correctly achieved. In 1869 the Joint Committee on Ordnance to the US Senate gave a chilling history of the Parrott and other guns adopted during the war; the most remarkable item was that 10 guns flew to pieces while lying on wooden chocks in the gunyard, before they had ever fired a shot, simply from residual stresses in the metal. And when the Union Navy undertook the bombardment of Fort Fisher in December 1864 every Parrott gun in the fleet burst sooner or later, killing and wounding 45 sailors; enemy fire from the fort only killed or wounded a further 11 men. For much of the time the Parrott guns were restricted to firing reduced charges in order to reduce the risk of accidents.

The Confederates acquired a number of Blakely rifles from England, and made good use of them, though even they failed spectacularly on occasion.

It will be recalled that Admiral Porter used barges carrying mortars to attack the forts at the mouth of the Mississippi River. These weapons were almost identical to those used by the Army,

Below: One of the hazards of hasty armament; a faulty gun explodes on board the USS *Carondelet* during the attack on Fort Donelson, 16 February 1862.

Right: A 10-inch mortar mounted in a gunboat for the bombardment of Fort Donelson.

13-inch caliber, short-barreled weapons firing enormous explosive shells. It was not possible to simply dump the mortar bed on to the deck of the barge or other ship and fire it; the whole vessel had to be strengthened by placing supporting timbers beneath the deck so as to distribute the recoil blow more evenly through the ship's structure. Providing this was done, though, and the 'bomb-ketch' was anchored in smooth water, surprisingly accurate shooting could be done at ranges up to about 4000 yards.

Mounting the bigger guns into ships became something of a problem. For generations the standard shipboard mounting had been the wooden 'truck carriage', a simple structure of two side cheeks supporting the gun trunnions, held securely by cross-transoms, and sitting on four small wheels. Elevation was achieved by driving in a 'quoin' or wedge between the carriage and the breech end of the gun; direction was given by heaving the carriage this way or that by ropes and pulleys. The wedge was marked in degrees, and the deck was similarly marked, so that the gun commander could apply elevation and direction as ordered. The pointing of such guns was so primitive that individual gun-laying was only possible when the ship was anchored and firing at a fixed target. When the ship was moving and firing at another ship there was no hope of being

Below: Probably the best-known depiction of the Battle of Hampton Roads is this Currier & Ives lithograph first published shortly after the event.

Above: Yet another artist's impression of the *Monitor* and *Virginia* battle, and perhaps the most technically accurate.

Below: The Union blockading fleet off Ship Island near the mouth of the Mississippi, with the USS *Mississippi* firing at a Confederate steamer.

able to point the gun at the enemy with sufficient accuracy to achieve a hit. What had to be resorted to was broadside fire in which every gun fired at once, on the orders of the gunnery officer. His task was to observe the enemy, estimate the range and direction, order it to the guns, then, as the ship began its upward roll, to order 'fire' at the right moment so that the shot would strike the enemy.

Once the gun fired, it and its carriage recoiled violently inboard. A 'breeching rope' passed through the hole in the cascable (the 'button' on the rear end of a muzzle-loading gun) and was attached to the ship's side. This, together with the friction of the wheels on their axles and the slope of the deck, helped to resist the recoil movement, but several tons of gun moving rapidly through a web of ropes and barefooted sailors made for some lively side-stepping.

The American solution was the invention of the Marsilly carriage. This resembled the truck carriage but did away with the two rear wheels,

allowing the body of the carriage to rest directly on the deck. Thus the recoil had to overcome the friction of the wooden carriage against the deck, which could be augmented by throwing a handful of sand on the deck. Once the gun was loaded, a handspike lever with a pair of small wheels could be thrust underneath the rear end of the carriage, and with two men bearing down on this the carriage was lifted slightly off the deck so that it could be trundled forward for firing.

The adoption of the heavy rifled guns brought problems, since they were far too big to be placed on Marsilly carriages. The solution adopted was much the same as the Army's carriage and slide adopted in fortifications. The gun was fitted into a carriage somewhat resembling a truck carriage but without the truck. This ran upon a slide, anchored to the deck by a pivot at the front end, but provided with rollers under the rear end to allow the slide, and hence the carriage and gun, to be swung from side to side by the use of rope and tackle. The carriage was fitted with small truck wheels: those at the front were continuously in contact with the slide, while those at the rear were on an eccentric axle and could be brought out of or into engagement. Instead of the Army style of compressor hanging beneath the slide, the Navy had to adopt a different pattern because there was very little space between the slide and the deck. Instead a screw jack at the side of the carriage squeezed in two plates against the side of the slide. This, together with friction from the carriage, served to control recoil and the eccentric wheels were thrown into contact for running the gun out to fire again.

Ammunition

Naval ammunition differed only slightly from army ammunition. Solid shot was used more, even with rifled guns, since its function was to smash through the iron armor on the opposing ship. There were two enemy schools of thought on this question. One was known as the 'racking' school, while the other group was described as the 'punching' party.

'Racking' meant hitting the enemy ship with the heaviest possible weight of shot, at a not particularly high velocity. The object in view was to 'rack' or strain the skeleton of the ship with repeated heavy blows so that the armor plating would be displaced and fall away and the structure of the ship be weakened and eventually broken. Even though such impacts against the armor would not penetrate, the force of the blow often fractured the wooden backing sufficiently to drive off splinters with considerable force, and these, flying into the crowded areas of the ship, dealt out fearsome injuries to the crew.

Left: A 10-inch Parrott gun on the Confederate gunboat *Teazer.* Note the eccentric wheels, the strong breeching rope and the tackles to help in pointing the gun.

Above: Two Confederate ironclads in Charleston Bay, with the city in the background. A painting by Conrad W Chapman.

'Punching' meant using a much smaller caliber of shot at the highest possible velocity in order to penetrate the armor plate and its backing and then ricochet around inside the ship to do damage to the men and guns.

In general, racking was the role of smooth-bore guns: they fired massive iron balls at low velocity to give enormous blows. The 15-inch Rodman, for example, fired a 453-pound solid shot at 1220 feet per second to give an impact force of 4285 foot-tons. One of these guns with this performance was tested by the British Ordnance Select Committee in 1867, against an armored target consisting of 4.5 inches of iron backed by 30 inches of teak. 'The iron plate was cracked and bent back, indented 14 inches by 13 inches. Depth of dent 4 inches. Several cracks in plate around indent. In rear, two ribs cracked and four bulged,' said the report.

In order to punch a way through the armor it was obvious that heavier shot and greater velocity would be needed, and here the theorists ran up against the fact that for a smooth-bore gun there was only one size and weight of shot. A 15-inch gun could take a 15-inch ball, no more and not much less, and the weight of a 15-inch sphere of iron settled the question of how heavy the shot was going to be. The only way to get a heavier shot to the enemy was to go for a bigger gun, which was why both Rodman and Dahlgren went for 20-inch designs. But increases in size brought their own problems; the 20-inch guns fired a 1080-pound ball, and the simple physical problem of getting this up to the muzzle and loading it was daunting. On tests the 20-inch Rodman took 8 minutes to load, and that was with a skilled crew on a proving ground. What it would take with a hastily trained volunteer crew, pitching up and down at sea and being shot at the while, was another question.

So the punching school devoted their attention to extracting as much performance as they could from rifled guns, because only rifled guns would permit the use of an elongated projectile and thus provide a heavier shot for any given caliber. As an example, we can consider the caliber of eight inches: the eight-inch smooth-bore in use by the Union Navy fired a 68-pound solid shot; the eight-inch Parrott fired a 152-pound solid shot. Even if the Parrott did not achieve the same velocity as the smooth-bore, there was still such a surplus of weight in the shot that its attack was bound to have greater force. Unfortunately the science of measuring velocity was then in its infancy and we have no figures on the eight-inch Parrott gun; but a comparable weapon, the British eight-inch rifled muzzle-loading Armstrong of 1866, when fired with a 180-pound shot, gave an average velocity of 1338 feet per second. If the Parrott, with a 152-pound shot, achieved the same velocity – and there is no reason why it should not have done – then it would have developed a muzzle energy of 1850 foot-tons. The smooth-bore eight-inch could only achieve 300 foot-tons.

Relative impact forces are not, however, the entire story. Without going into the mathematics, it can be shown that much of the effect on the target is due to the greater velocity which the rifled gun can bring to bear. In effect, with a low velocity the target yields and has time to adapt itself to the impact; with a high velocity the shot tears through the plate before it has time to yield.

Although the full scientific explanations for the superiority of the punching method of attack were not to be understood for several years after the war, there was nevertheless a sufficient amount of evidence from actual firing to show that the rifled gun had the advantage, particularly at short ranges where its additional velocity was still evident. Moreover, there was one irrefutable argument for the punching school: they were attacking the target behind the armor, while the racking school were attacking the armor.

Explosive shells used by the Navy also had one important difference: they did not carry fuzes. The Navy wanted the shell to burst on impact and, as we have already seen, impact fuzes and round shells do not go together. But in their case there was no need for a fuze. The shell was filled with gunpowder and plugged; when it struck the target the impact was so violent that the gunpowder, thrown about in the shell, exploded from the friction with the rough shell interior and the high impact force. When rifled guns came into use the same rule applied, and again there was no requirement to complicate matters with fuzes. It was not until several years after the war, when the

Below: The Battle of New Orleans, 24 April 1862. A painting by J O Davidson.

Above: Admiral David Glasgow Farragut of New Orleans fame; a photograph by Matthew Brady.

Left: A young 'powder monkey' of the Union Navy leans against his 8-inch Parrott gun. Note the racks of cutlasses in the background, for defense against boarders.

Right: A moored torpedo. If the firing lever 'E' is depressed by a ship moving downstream (left to right), nothing happens; if it is forced upwards by a ship moving upstream it fires the explosive charge.

advances in technology had provided them with shells which would completely penetrate the side of the enemy ship, that it became necessary to devise fuzes which would detonate the shell after it had gone through the armor.

The other difference in Navy ammunition lay in the method of firing the guns. The Army's friction primer had been tried when it was first invented, but was soon discarded, for a very practical reason. Once the gun had fired, the gunner shook the serrated pin off the end of his lanyard, preparatory to hooking the lanyard on to the next primer. The discarded pin fell to the floor, where it became a hazard for the barefoot sailors running about. So the Navy adopted a simpler form of primer, resembling a nail. The shank was filled with powder and inserted into the vent of the gun, while the head was filled with percussion cap composition. A hammer was hinged to the top of the gun and operated by pulling a lanyard, so that the head of the hammer fell on the head of the primer and fired it. The axis of the hammer was slotted, so that the last movement of the lanyard, after the primer had been struck, pulled the hammer head off the top of the primer. This was done because the explosion pressure, rushing back up the vent, would blow out the empty primer body, and if the hammer was resting on the top of the primer it would be flung back with sufficient force to break.

Mines and Torpedoes

When Admiral Farragut led the expedition into New Orleans, he went down in history for his cry of 'Damn the torpedoes, full speed ahead!' But the things he was damning were not the torpedoes we know today. The self-propelled torpedo had not been invented at the time of the Civil War; the danger to Farragut's fleet came from what we would call mines.

The idea of placing explosive charges into the water so that an enemy would run against them was old by the time the Civil War began, and the Americans had used crude mines against the British in 1776. By 1860 the invention of the percussion cap had made the ignition of such devices somewhat easier, and several designs were put forward. In the main, the mine was favored more by the Confederates; it was an ideal weapon for a weaker naval power, which the Confederates certainly were, and moreover it was particularly applicable to riverine warfare at that stage of the mine's development. The technology which would allow reliable mines to be laid in deep sea was nowhere in sight.

The mine – or torpedo, as we must call it for the purposes of this study – has a twofold advantage. In the first place it will destroy or seriously damage ships, particularly the wooden ships of the period. In the second place it has a powerful effect on the sailor's mind; if he knows – or even only suspects – that a stretch of water is sown with torpedoes, then he is likely to be cautious in his

Right: One of the 'David' torpedo boats being prepared for action in Charleston Harbor. A painting by Conrad W Chapman.

approach. Not every sailor was as forthright and bold as Farragut.

The simplest torpedoes were those planted in fixed positions in stretches of water where attack might be expected. Such a device might be a canister of gunpowder attached to the top of a wooden stake. The bottom of the stake was connected to an iron weight by a short chain, while another, longer, chain and weight were attached to the stake close to the canister. At the top of the canister would be a ring of simple firing devices consisting of soft metal blisters with firing pins

Below: A Confederate working party laying torpedoes at night in the harbor channel off Charleston.

Above: The USS *Kearsarge* sinking the Confederate blockade runner *Alabama* outside the harbor of Cherbourg, France, 19 June 1864.

and percussion caps inside. The 'stake torpedo' was dropped into the water so that the end weight anchored the stake in place, and the second weight and longer chain would hold the stake at a suitable angle, pointed toward the enemy's line of approach. Obviously, selecting the depth of water and length of stake was fairly critical, and this kind of torpedo could easily be tailored for a particular location. Once in place the torpedo stayed there until an approaching ship knocked against the percussion cap holders on the canister, whereupon the charge, perhaps 50 pounds of gunpowder, would explode. As with all underwater explosive devices, much of the effect was due to the resistance of the water; when the charge exploded in proximity to a ship, the tendency was for the water to direct the blast to the ship, which was the weaker structure.

Right: Rear Admiral Raphael Semmes, CSN, captain of the *Alabama*, from a photograph taken in England after the loss of his ship.

For completely barring a river or creek, a framework of wood could be set up under the water, with strong stakes pointing downstream. At the head of each stake a simple artillery shell, complete with an armed percussion fuze, was attached. This meant an explosive device perhaps every two or three feet across the width of the stream, so that there was no chance of an enemy evading them.

Where the water was deeper, so that a stake torpedo became an ungainly article, the canister would simply be anchored to a suitable weight and would be only partially filled with explosive so as to leave a buoyancy chamber with sufficient displacement to make the torpedo float at the limit of its anchor chain. Again percussion devices would be fitted to the top in sufficient number to ensure that, no matter how the ship struck the device, one of the caps was bound to fire.

Right: A variety of Confederate torpedoes. At the top is a diagram of the 'David' torpedo boats, showing how the spar torpedo was carried. (6) shows the Confederate submarine *Hunley*.

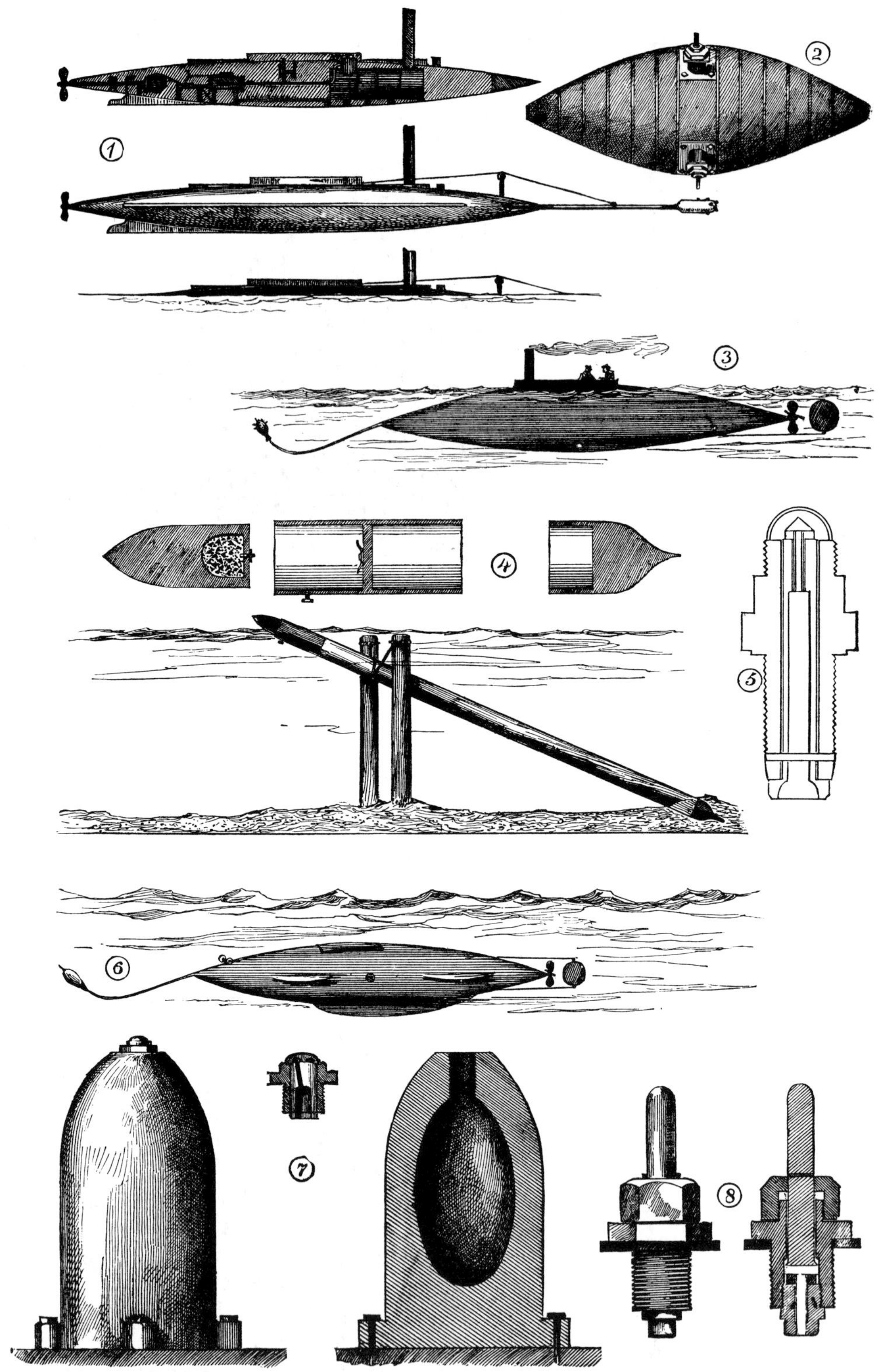

DRAWN BY E. T. MEEKER, FROM SKETCHES BY HORATIO L. WAIT.

1. CONFEDERATE TORPEDO-BOAT "DAVID." 2. CONFEDERATE TORPEDO. 3. CONFEDERATE TORPEDO-BOAT, AS DESCRIBED BY A REFUGEE. 4. CONFEDERATE SPAR-TORPEDO. 5. FUSE OF A BARREL-TORPEDO FOUND IN THE ST. JOHN'S RIVER. 6. CONFEDERATE SUBMARINE TORPEDO-BOAT, AS DESCRIBED BY A REFUGEE. 7. CONFEDERATE VOLCANO-TORPEDO. 8. CONFEDERATE TORPEDO-FUSE.

Awareness of torpedoes meant that captains would send a small boat ahead to peer into the water and see if they could detect any mysterious devices lying in wait. If they did they could gently rope the thing and haul it up to where it could be seen and dealt with, either by unscrewing the ignition device or, more often, simply placing a charge on it, rowing briskly away and waiting for it to blow up harmlessly. To counter this sort of move the 'Turtle' torpedo was invented. This was a simple hemispherical iron container of explosive fitted with a pull-release firing pin and attached to a moored torpedo by a length of line. Should anyone attempt to haul up the moored torpedo, the firing mechanism of the Turtle would be released, under the boat of the pulling-up party with any luck.

Mechanical firing devices were used on several designs. One Confederate river torpedo moored a five-foot cylinder of explosive under the water, with an articulated lever protruding close to the surface. A ship passing downriver would merely depress the lever harmlessly, but any ship moving upriver would force the lever in the opposite direction, cocking and releasing a firing pin against a percussion cap to fire the charge.

An ingenious design was Singer's Torpedo, a moored device. This was a buoyant canister of explosive with a firing pin already cocked and held back by a pin. The pin had a line attached, and this ran to a heavy weight loosely fitted on top of the explosive container. Any ship hitting the torpedo would displace the weight, and as this fell through the water it would pull out the safety pin, so releasing the firing mechanism. This, of course, was only applicable to fairly calm waters, where the firing weight would not be displaced by wave motion.

The application of electricity as a firing method was first tried during the Civil War. It had been discovered that electric current applied through a fine wire would heat the wire sufficiently to ignite gunpowder, and this was used as a method of firing moored torpedoes. A pattern of torpedoes would be laid in a stretch of water, all connected by cable to an observing post on shore. Various markers, either innocent-appearing debris floating in the water or aiming devices sited on the shore, would identify the position of each torpedo. When the enemy flotilla sailed in, the observers would watch their designated spot and if a ship passed over it they would connect the wire to a storage battery and so ignite the torpedo. Unfortunately the science of electricity was in its infancy, and this system failed as many times as it succeeded, doubtless because the torpedo firing squad failed to take into account the resistance of the length of wire, with the result that insufficient electricity would reach the torpedo to set it off. It is said that during a Union attack on Charleston,

Below: A typical moored torpedo, found in the Potomac River by the paddle-steamer *Resolute*.

South Carolina, the USS *New Ironsides* paused for some time over a torpedo containing several thousand pounds of gunpowder, but in spite of several attempts to fire, it failed to operate.

Another method of attack, usually against a flotilla which had appeared in a river, was simply to throw buoyant torpedoes into the water and allow the current to carry them down against the enemy. These simple devices would be studded with percussion cap firing mechanisms so that they would explode as soon as they struck anything. Somewhat more ambitious was a Confederate design which had a spring firing pin restrained by a cross-bolt attached to a screwed rod upon which was a propeller. Thrown into the water the entire torpedo would drift, and the propeller would remain stationary. As soon as the torpedo was stopped, as by coming up against a ship, the flow of the current, continuing past the torpedo, would rotate the propeller and, because of the screwed rod, withdraw the cross-bolt, so allowing the firing pin to operate. This device had the advantage that if the torpedo struck some floating debris and was merely checked momentarily, it would not explode but would float free and continue until it struck something sufficiently robust to halt it.

To carry the war more actively to the enemy, the 'spar torpedo' was adopted. This was a canister of explosive attached to a long wooden spar and fitted either with a percussion firing device or with a firing pin mechanism controlled by a line. The spar was attached to a small boat and the line, if one was used, led into the boat. The boat's crew now sailed toward the enemy, preferably at night when they were unlikely to be seen, and as they got close the spar torpedo would be lowered so that the explosive canister was in the water some twenty or more feet ahead of the boat. Eventually the attacking boat was close enough for the torpedo to strike the enemy ship below the waterline, whereupon it fired itself or a member of the boat's crew pulled the line and fired it. One might expect that the spar would be projected backwards with some force, and in any event, being twenty to thirty feet away from a heavy charge of powder exploding must have been a daunting experience. In spite of the hazards, though, the spar torpedo was frequently used in action, and it survived in other navies until the 1880s. The Confederate ram *Albemarle* was sunk with a spar torpedo placed by a small boat in this manner.

The Confederate Navy, seeing the advantages of the spar torpedo provided it could be got into position effectively, went so far as to devise a new type of warship for the task. These became known as 'Davids', from the analogy with David

Right: The explosion of a Confederate torpedo under the bows of the Union gunboat *Commodore Barney* on the James River, 4 August 1863. 30 men were swept overboard, all but two of whom were saved, and it was possible to tow the wounded ship to harbor.

The USS *Sassacus* (left) in action with the Confederate ironclad *Albemarle* in May 1864.

and Goliath, and were small steam-propelled craft of cigar-like shape. They were provided with ballast tanks so that when approaching the enemy they could take on water and thus sink down until only a small pilot-house was visible above the surface; this was painted blue-gray in order to make it as inconspicuous as possible. A long spar was attached to the bow of the vessel, carrying a canister with about 100 pounds of gunpowder and a percussion firing device. The David simply set its course for the Union target, sank into the water, and then drove as hard as it could until the torpedo struck and exploded. It then backed away and sailed off, relying upon its tiny exposed area to preserve it from any retaliation. Davids had some success in Charleston harbor at different times.

One might conclude that from the 'David' it was but a short step to making a vessel which would submerge completely, but the transition was extremely difficult and was only achieved once. Again, it was the Confederate Navy which put the CSS *Hunley* to sea, a true submarine. Invented by Horace L Hunley, this vessel was largely based on an old boiler; it was 25 feet long and was propelled through the water by a screw driven by hand cranks from inside the boat, turned by the eight-man crew. The captain, at a conning tower in the forward end, controlled a rudder and also two horizontal fins which enabled the *Hunley* to dive and surface. There were two conning towers, one at each end, sealed by hatches and with glass ports to allow the captain to see, as best he could, where he was going. Ballast tanks were fitted to enable the craft to submerge until its upper surface was just under the water. The crew then applied themselves to the crank, generating a speed of just over three knots in calm water, and the captain operated the horizontal fins to make the boat dive. The usual spar torpedo was attached to the front of the boat, and the method of operation was that of the David: go for the enemy until the torpedo struck and exploded.

The *Hunley* had a patchy history. During her initial trials she sank three times, drowning her crew on each occasion, Hunley himself being among the victims. But eventually all the problems were solved, another crew found, and the boat was made to work reasonably well. Eventually the *Hunley's* day of fame arrived, and, crewed by Lieutenant George E Dixon and six men, she sailed beneath the waters of Charleston harbor to place her torpedo fairly and squarely against the USS *Housatonic*. In the subsequent explosion both ships were destroyed.

Although we have said that the self-propelled torpedo had not been invented, there was at least one attempt to do so. In December 1862 a Mr Pascal Plant offered the Union Navy his 'rocket-propelled submarine torpedo' for trial. Two of these devices were duly fired from a barge moored on the Potomac River. One dived into the mud and exploded, the other suddenly veered off at 60 degrees to the line of fire and sank a small schooner, the proverbial innocent bystander, which thus has the dubious distinction of being the first ship ever to be sunk by a self-propelled torpedo. Nothing daunted, Plant arranged a second demonstration early in 1863; this was apparently no better, and with that the Union's interest in mobile torpedoes ceased.

GEN'L HAUPT.

5
THE SUPPORTING SERVICES

Previous page: The locomotive *General Haupt* of the US Military Railroads, at the Alexandria roundhouse, 1863.

The Railroads

The American Civil War broke new ground in several directions, and not merely in the technology of weapons. With upwards of two million men mobilized and a theater of war of many thousands of square miles, supplying, maintaining and transporting these forces demanded considerable innovative efforts, commanding them effectively placed demands upon generalship which found many professional soldiers wanting, and the economic direction of the war effort imposed strains on the community which had never been foreseen. In many respects this background to the war can prove far more interesting than the most stirring battle.

One of the keys to the Civil War was transportation. It is generally held that this was the first conflict in which the railroad played an important role. This is not exactly true, since the European nations had begun exploring the relationship between railroads and warfare many years before. As early as 1830 the British Government had experimented with moving troops by rail, and in 1842 a Prussian theorist had published *The Railway Exemplified as a Military Operational Line* which pointed out the likelihood of Prussia having to fight on two fronts – Russia and France – and postulated the desirability of planning railroad lines so that in addition to serving the population's day-to-day needs, they would also be ideally sited to serve as rapid transit channels for the movement of troops to one or other threatened front or from one front to the other. Whether this text was heeded is unknown, but within three years lines were being built to the two frontiers and in 1846 the Prussian Army moved 12,000 men with horses and guns from Potsdam to Posen by rail in record time.

The first actual use of railways in war came with the French invasion of Italy in 1859, when in a period of 86 days the French moved over 600,000 men and 129,000 horses to concentrate their armies on the Italian border. This remarkable feat was somewhat marred by the speed with which it outstripped the remainder of the French administrative system, since, in practice, what happened was that trainloads of men and horses were suddenly deposited in out-of-the-way places and left to wait for their ammunition, rations and other supplies to catch up with them. This was a lesson in organization which took some time to learn.

At the outbreak of the Civil War there were about 22,000 miles of railroad in the North and some 9000 miles in the Southern states. During the course of the war a further 4000 miles were built in the North, but very little in the South. In addition, the lines in the North were in better condition than those in the South, both in the

Below: Recognizing the vulnerability of their communications to raiding parties, the Union army installed gun batteries at strategic points on the railroad system.

track and in the quality and quantity of equipment. The ownership of lines in both North and South was spread among a multitude of private companies, management was conducted on simple principles, and little or no progress had been made on standardizing either equipment or operating practices. Even the gage of the track was not standardized in 1861, so that the flexibility of rail communication that we know today, with through routes and interchangeability of equipment, was totally unknown. Railroads operated to the limit of their corporate boundary; this frequently meant arriving in a depot at one side of a city or town, after which the freight and passengers had to be moved across town by wagon to the depot of the next railroad for continuation of the journey.

The Union was well supplied with foundries and factories to produce the equipment necessary for railroad construction, maintenance and operation. On the other hand the Confederacy had very few facilities in this field other than the Tredegar Iron Works in Richmond, and various small concerns in Nashville, Atlanta, Augusta and Centerville, Georgia. For this reason very few new locomotives were added to the Southern railroads during the war, most of their 'new' motive power being acquired by capturing locomotives in raids on the Union railroads.

Moreover, there was a much greater diversity of rail gages in the Southern states, and all the Southern locomotives were wood-burners, a condition which remained throughout the war. By contrast, coal-burning locomotives had been introduced in the North as recently as 1859, and by 1865 the conversion to coal by Northern railroads was complete. This poor state of development of the Southern railroads, together with the effects of the Union blockade, made logistics a particularly difficult problem for the Confederacy throughout the war, and the record of the Southern lines is one of considerable ingenuity in the face of great odds.

As it happened, the layout of the railroads within the Southern states was well suited to defense. There was a continuous line across the northern boundary of the Confederacy, made up of connecting lines of various companies, which extended from Alexandria, Virginia, through Lynchburg and Roanoke, then along the southern border of Tennessee to Memphis. From Memphis another line carried on down to New Orleans, 400 miles away. Along the Atlantic seacoast lines ran continuously from Fredericksburg through Richmond and Petersburg, Wilmington, Charleston and Savannah for 650 miles, and connecting lines carried this system into South Georgia and then into Florida and on to the Gulf of Mexico. Thus the South was enclosed on three sides with a more or less continuous line of some 2000 miles which was of considerable strategic

Right: The railroad depot at Nashville, Tennessee, with locomotives of the US Military Railroads.

Right: The First Battle of Bull Run, 21 July 1861, which was decisively influenced by the arrival of Confederate reinforcements by railroad.

value, and, with their connecting lines providing interior routes, these railroads were capable of moving Confederate troops in virtually any direction to meet a perceived threat.

The Northern lines fell into two broad groups: those which, remote from the theaters of war, were simply involved in 'business as usual', though rather more of it than they were accustomed to; and those closer to the scenes of conflict which were to be more concerned with movements of troops and supplies and which therefore played a more vital part in the conduct of the war. To give but one example of the problems faced by private railroads, we can cite the

Right: Building a replacement bridge to carry the Orange & Alexandria Railroad across Bull Run Creek near Union Mills.

Right: A pontoon bridge replaces a wrecked railroad bridge across a Southern river.

dilemma facing the Baltimore and Ohio line when the war began. A considerable proportion of this company's railroad lay in the Potomac River valley, where it became part of the combat zone, particularly that stretch between Harper's Ferry and Martinsburg, across the Shenandoah Valley. At the outbreak of war the president of the line was threatened with having his railroad confiscated by the Governor of Virginia if it was used to transport Federal troops to Washington, while at the same time the Secretary of the Interior threatened him with indictment for treason if he *refused* to carry Federal troops into Washington.

The first major battle of the war, variously known as Bull Run or Manassas, took place on 21st July 1861. The Manassas Gap Railroad was used to carry Confederate troops of General Joseph E Johnston to reinforce those of General P T Beauregard, and it was the arrival, by train, of General T J Jackson's Confederate brigade

Right: The 14th Wisconsin Volunteers charging a New Orleans battery at the Battle of Shiloh, 7 April 1862.

Right: A Confederate raiding party tearing up a stretch of track so as to disrupt the Union supply system.

which turned what could have been a Confederate defeat into a victory. This served to show how vital good rail communication could be to the outcome of the war, but an even more lucid example can be seen in the sequence of events which followed the Union capture of Corinth, Mississippi, on 30th May 1862.

In February 1862 Grant had captured Fort

Right: The other side of the coin: Union troops destroy a Confederate railroad line. Notice the simple and effective tactic of heating the rails on a fire until soft, then wrapping them round a convenient tree.

Henry, on the Tennessee River, and Fort Donelson on the Cumberland River. This forced the Confederates to pull back their line of defense to new locations south of the Cumberland River, and in so doing they exposed the entire line of the Memphis and Charleston Railroad to attack. In March, Grant moved up the Tennessee River and fought the indecisive Battle of Shiloh. Subsequent Union advances led to the Confederates giving up Corinth, to withdraw some 50 miles down the Mobile and Ohio line to Tupelo, Mississippi. Thus the line of the Memphis and Charleston Railroad, the eastern terminus of which was Chattanooga, was lost to the Confederates for the rest of the war, depriving the South of its only continuous line of communication from the Mississippi River to the Atlantic Coast and on, north, to the vital battle zone of Northern Virginia. Chattanooga now became the bastion of the outer line of Confederate defense, capable of being supplied by a line running south through Atlanta and Montgomery to Mobile Bay, and a line running eastward through Knoxville to Richmond and Alexandria. The Union capture of Knoxville cut this line, leaving upper Georgia and western North Carolina virtually defenseless and reducing the South to one main line for supply.

Once the vulnerability of railroads was appreciated – the ease with which rails could be ripped up, and rolling stock derailed – raids were conducted by both sides with increasing frequency, though the Confederates were the greatest protagonists of this form of warfare. This was due to strategic considerations: the Union wanted to preserve railroads in Confederate territory so as to be able to make use of them after their capture, whereas the Confederates were simply concerned with being as destructive as possible in order to upset the Union's supply routes.

The greatest upheaval in railroad operation came about because, at the outset, neither the railroads nor the Governments had any idea of what operating a railroad in wartime entailed. In the beginning the railroads handled military traffic just as they would have handled any commercial traffic, moving soldiers and suppliers on the same trains which handled commercial passengers and shipments and hence subjecting them to the same delays. But whereas commercial traffic at that time was mainly short-haul, troop movements and military supplies largely became long-haul matters and this brought into sharp focus the various problems stemming from the diversity of gages, the different ownerships, the differing operating practices and the inadequate arrangements for transhipment of passengers and freight from one line to another. But within days of the attack on Fort Sumter, President Lincoln had, far-sightedly, signed an order setting up in effect a US Military Railway Service

Below: General Haupt supervising a Union construction crew at Devereaux Station on the Orange & Alexandria Railroad, 1863.

Right: General Herman Haupt, Superintendent of Eastern Railroads.

with powers of virtual seizure over all Northern lines. In fact very little was done to implement the powers contained in this order for some time, the Government preferring to rely upon the co-operation and public spirit of the individual managements, but when it appeared that these faculties were beginning to wane, there was no hesitation in putting military appointees into places where they could do the most good.

In August 1861 Thomas Scott, Vice-President of the Pennsylvania Railroad, was made Assistant Secretary of War with special responsibility for military control of railroads. Scott resigned within a short time, but not before he had achieved the appointment of D C McCallum, General Superintendent of the Erie Railroad, as Military Director and Superintendent of Railroads in the West, with the rank of colonel, later advanced to brigadier. Shortly afterward Herman Haupt, a young engineer who later had a prominent technical career, was commissioned to assume similar responsibilities for the Eastern railroads. Haupt was given his colonel's commission in April 1862 after McDowell's advance on Richmond had discovered the line of the Richmond, Fredericksburg & Potomac Railroad to have been comprehensively destroyed by the retreating Confederates. The Union had been relying upon this line for their future supply, and Colonel Haupt was given the formidable task of assembling a construction force and rebuilding the line, which he astonished everyone by doing inside three weeks. Among the feats performed by Haupt's force was the building of a 400-foot long, 100-foot high bridge across the Potomac Creek in nine days, which led one disgruntled Confederate to say: 'Them Yankees can build bridges faster than us Rebels can burn 'em down.'

Below: The Potomac Creek Bridge, Richmond Fredericksburg & Potomac RR, built by Haupt's construction crews in nine days, May 1862.

The problems and struggles continued until Sherman's famous 'March to the Sea' in December 1864. Here, for the first time, was a Union force not concerned with preserving the railroads it encountered, since Sherman had no intention of occupying the ground through which he was advancing. All that he needed was a single line of track up which his supplies could come, and this his force laid as it advanced, so that supplies came from a base some 360 miles behind in sufficient quantity to sustain his army of 100,000 men and 60,000 horses. Sherman maneuvered into a position to strike from behind the Confederate line of defense and finally cut the tenuous rail link which held the South together, the line between Charleston and Savannah. The final strategic blow came in April 1865 when Union troops raided into Virginia and captured the important junction of Petersburg. This severed the final supply line and was instrumental in bringing about the surrender of General Lee a few days later.

The operation of American railroads was facilitated by the development of the electric telegraph and the invention and universal adoption of the Morse code. Alongside every stretch of track was its associated telegraph line, and every station was connected with the headquarters of the line so that 'Train Orders' could be transmitted to control the movement of all rolling stock. At that time almost the entire rail system of the US was single track, demanding rigorous control of movement so that two trains moving in opposite directions never got on to the same stretch of track. This was achieved by unambiguous orders, sent by telegraph, directing trains to move or stand still according to an overall plan prepared by despatchers. At the same time the telegraph conveyed the commercial business of the railroad, demands for rolling stock to carry freight, reports of defects in stock, notices of lateness of trains, every sort of information necessary to the functioning of the line. Even the local time was controlled in this way, the stationmaster relying upon the noon time signal from the railroad and thus acting as the timekeeper for the whole community.

Such a useful network was obviously of considerable value to the military forces, who were quick to put the railroad telegraph to even more use than they put the railroads themselves. And having seen the speed and precision with which orders could be so despatched, it was but a short step from there to setting up an entirely military telegraph system.

Below: The railroads were operated far beyond their designed limits, and this resulted in frequent derailments due to track spreading beneath the excessive traffic. These troops were Confederate reinforcements for General Jackson in Mississippi.

Left: A group of engineers of the US Military Railroad Construction Corps, with a selection of their tools and surveying instruments, in Chattanooga, 1864.

Below: A visual signal station operated by Union troops.

The Signal Corps

The first organized military communication system was formed by the Confederates, who set up a Corps of Signallers under E P Alexander, later Confederate Chief of Artillery. This formed part of the Adjutant-General's Department and was responsible for communications and also for espionage and counter-espionage. The Union Army, strangely, had considerable difficulty in setting up a Corps of Signallers, due principally to internal disputes in the War Department as to who should have responsibility. It was not until August 1864 that the Signal Corps US Army became a separate unit; until then it was the neglected stepchild of the infantry, artillery,

Right: A visual signal station in operation, using torches in poor visibility instead of flags.

engineers or the quartermaster corps as the political wind blew.

The US Military Telegraph Corps was separate from the US Signal Corps, principally because its operations were mainly in the hinterland rather than in the front line and most of its operators were civilians. This led to some friction between the Telegraph Corps and the military commanders, because the Corps was answerable only to the War Department and was independent of local commanders, who had absolutely no powers over it. The commercial telegraph lines in the East were taken over by government decree in April 1861. The formation of independent com-

Right: A military telegraph wagon unloading, prior to setting up a field telegraph station.

Right: Laying a telegraph line during a battle; this was the responsibility of the Signal Corps, but in fact cable was rarely laid this far forward.

panies of telegraphists in the West, organized by General Fremont, was strongly opposed by the private companies, who, in spite of the war, could only see the rise of a possible competitor and threw every objection in their way. Fremont, under political pressure, had to give way and disband his companies, but sense prevailed and in April 1862 Congress passed legislation enabling the Army to take over all private telegraph companies, and the railroad telegraph systems, throughout the United States.

With this legislation secure, the Military Telegraph Corps then began to build its own system to extend and augment the commercial lines. Direct lines were laid from Washington to the principal Army headquarters, so that orders went directly to Army commanders. From the Army HQ lines were then laid to the headquarters of Corps, and the field crews made sure that whenever Corps moved, so the line accompanied them and that communication back to Army was maintained.

Forward of Corps, to divisions and regiments, the communication network was less formal. Here the Signal Corps assumed greater responsibility and the system broke into two different methods, telegraphy and visual communication. Telegraphy was used where the front was fairly static, and went as far forward as was practicable. But for the most part, and particularly when formations were moving frequently, visual communication was adopted, since a line of communication could be established easily and quickly and could be kept functioning during most of a move.

While flares and lights had their uses, the principal system was flag signalling. At this time the semaphore system – using flags held at different angles to the signaller's body – appears not to have been developed, and the application of Morse code to flag signalling was also unknown. The flag signallers therefore adopted a system which, so far as the individual went, was very simple but which required a somewhat involved infrastructure. All the signaller had to know was

Right: An office of the Military Telegraph Corps at a Corps headquarters in the field.

Above: A field telegraph station manned by Signal Corps personnel, with the Army of the Potomac in 1864.

Right: The Heart of the Network: the Central Signal Station, Washington DC, April 1865. From here visual and telegraph communications stretched to all the field armies.

three positions of his flag: starting with the flag held upright in front of his face, he moved the flag in a semicircle down to his left to indicate the figure 1; or down and to his right to indicate the figure 2; or down and forward, to his feet, to indicate the figure 3. Thus all the signaller had to memorize was three movements, rather than the 36 combinations of dots (right) and dashes (left) which constituted the Morse alphabet and figures and which future generations of military signallers had to memorize.

But to construct sensible messages with only three digits meant backing up the signaller with a code-book in which combinations of these figures were used to represent letters, words or phrases. Thus '1.1' represented 'A'; '2.2.2' represented 'Y'; '2.1.1.1.2' asked 'Are you ready to receive?'; '2.2.1.1.1' asked 'Do you understand?'; '3' meant 'End of word' while '3.3' signalled 'End of message'. In general, messages were sent in combinations of 1 and 2, while 3 was reserved for procedural signals.

The drawback with visual signalling is, of course, that it is visible to anyone with eyes to see and a suitable position from which to observe. The simple code given above was probably sufficient to conceal the message from casual watchers, but anyone with determination could fairly easily unravel the system and read the messages. Because of this, more complication was introduced in the shape of military codes and ciphers. By modern standards these were 'low level' ciphers; perhaps the most usual was the 'cipher wheel', two concentric discs, one smaller than the other, with alphabets inscribed around their edges. The two alphabets were jumbled, and useful items as 'End of word' and the common endings '-tion' and '-ing' were also included. By revolving the discs so that some prearranged combination was set – for example, 'End of word' might be set opposite to 'D' – the letters of the message were looked up on one disc and the corresponding cipher letter taken from the other, until the message was constructed. The recipient, knowing the setting of the disc, would simply start on the 'cipher' alphabet and read backward to the 'clear' alphabet to read the message.

Given sufficient of these messages and a certain amount of time, breaking this type of cipher is not difficult. The Union Army appreciated this point and was able to break Confederate ciphers fairly readily, though the Confederates appear to have been much less successful. To protect against this, both sides would change their cipher settings at frequent intervals. Broadly speaking, if the orders contained in a message are for immediate execution, then even if the cipher is broken in due course little harm can result, since the action is completed before the enemy knows the content of the message. For messages with longer-term significance – orders for future strategic deployment, strength returns, intelligence reports and so forth – ciphers were held not to be sufficiently secure, and codes were used instead.

The code differs from the cipher. In the cipher, as we have seen, individual letters are transposed. In the code, whole words are transposed by means of a code-book which lists all the

KEEP OFF
THIS STATION

probable words necessary and allots each a distinct combination of letters or figures. In cipher the word 'stop' might be 'xnhw', but because of the nature of cipher the word 'pots' would therefore read 'whnx'. In code, 'stop' might be 'xnhw' but 'pots' might be 'kipg'. Thus decoding a message was impossible unless the recipient held a copy of the code-book, which was of course carefully guarded. Given sufficient time, codes can be broken, but the sophistication of code-breaking in the 1860s was not to present-day standards and thus codes were generally secure unless the code-book was stolen or lost.

The Balloon Corps

One of the more unusual applications of the telegraph system was upward, to a balloon. The Civil War was not the first military application of balloons, but it was certainly the first effective use of such a device in warfare. A gentleman called Thaddeus Lowe, a celebrated balloonist of prewar days, set about organizing a balloon corps in the summer of 1861 and offered its services to the Union Army. By January 1862 Lowe's corps was functioning with seven balloons and accompanied McClellan in the Peninsula campaign. Each balloon was supported by a mobile gas generator, using sulphuric acid and iron filings to generate hydrogen gas, and a squad of men to maintain it, fill it with gas and attend to the tethering ropes. McClellan authorized an extension from the Corps terminal of the Military Telegraph, and this was run to the balloon sites and then, by a trailing wire, actually into the basket of the balloon, so that the observers could telegraph back information immediately.

The original intention was purely to provide a super-elevated observation post, gaining the advantage of command over a longer distance. Thus the observers could see deep into enemy territory – or far in advance of the army – and report upon movements and concentrations. That this worked is in no doubt. The Confederates soon learned to keep their movements to a minimum when balloons were in the air, and one Confederate general observed that they were worth their keep for their nuisance value alone.

It soon became apparent that if men could observe from balloons, they could also spot the fall of shot from artillery fire and so direct fire into places which could not be seen by a ground observer. Observations could be taken on the fall of shot relative to the target and sent to the battery by telegraph, if the Signal Corps could be persuaded to lay the necessary linking line, or, what was more usual, simple visual signals from the balloon could be read by the battery, using a telescope, and acted upon. All the battery wanted to know was whether the shot had fallen right or left, over or short, and it did not take much sophistication to arrange a suitable system for signalling these four possibilities. Note that what

Right: A section of the Balloon Corps accompanying McClellan in the Peninsula in 1862. The box-like structures are hydrogen gas generators, feeding through a pressure regulator to fill the balloon.

Above: An observer takes to the air in a balloon early in 1862. His ascent is controlled by the men on the ropes, so that he gains sufficient altitude but is safe from drifting in the wind.

the balloonist reported were his observations; from these, the gun battery endeavored to make corrections to bring the shot on to the target. It was to be a long time, in any army, before the front line observer was actually permitted to order corrections to the guns; in the 1860s artillery were jealous of their expertise and were not going to allow any outsider to be party to the mysteries of gunnery. The idea of putting up a qualified artillery officer and allowing him to correct fire appears not to have been contemplated.

The Balloon Corps was another itinerant stepchild. McClellan first placed it under the control of the Corps of Topographic Engineers, since map-making seemed to be an obvious application. Then its connection with the Military Telegraph Corps was severed and it was allowed its own telegraph section, which was responsible for making the required connections to the military system. Then it was transferred to the Quartermaster's Department, and after a short period to the Corps of Engineers. Finally, early in 1863, it was handed over to the Signal Corps. They, short-handed already and with their strength fully stretched to provide communications, complained to the War Department that they could provide no men, nor did they have financial allocations which would permit them to run the balloons. This was the last straw as far as the War Department was concerned, and in May 1863 the Balloon Corps was disbanded.

The Confederates, seeing the utility of a balloon, decided to set up an observation unit. They, however, were severely hampered by the lack of specialist matériel. One balloon was made, of silk reputedly salvaged from dresses donated by the ladies of the South. There was not a sufficient supply of acid or iron to permit generation of hydrogen, so it was decided to anchor the balloon to a locomotive, then fill it with town gas, then drive the locomotive to a suitable spot from which observation could be made. This cumbersome system appears to have worked until, in a fit of ambition, the balloon was transferred from its locomotive to a steamboat in order to permit the aerial observer to take up a particular viewpoint. This worked once or twice, but eventually the captain of the steamboat miscalculated and ran aground, whereupon the boat and balloon were both captured by a Union patrol.

The Engineer Corps

At the outbreak of war the United States Army had two very professional engineer units. The Corps of Engineers was responsible for the construction of permanent fortifications, for the building and maintenance of nationally important communications such as waterways, canals, harbors and roads, the construction and repair of bridges, and the undertaking of other peacetime civil engineering projects as decided by the Government. This peacetime function continues to this day, it might be said, and the Corps of Engineers has been responsible for some exceptionally important construction during its lifetime. The wartime function of the Corps might be said to be the same as the peacetime, but in conditions of greater extemporization. Thus it was responsible for the construction of field fortifications for the armies, for the staking out of defensive lines to be excavated by other troops, for the preparation of emergency and pontoon bridges to cross water obstacles, for operating ferries to carry troops forward, for conducting various forms of technical reconnaissance, and generally for any sort of construction or engineering requirement which the field armies needed.

The Corps of Topographical Engineers was a separate entity, responsible, as the name implies, for surveying and the production of maps in the field. In fact the responsibilities of the two corps overlapped and mingled, so that in 1863 the logical step was taken and the Topographical Engineers were merged into the Corps of Engineers. The survey function was vital to the

Below: A party of topographical engineers at work preparing maps in 1862.

progress of the war; much of the area over which the war was fought had never been properly mapped, and the Topographical Engineers were the first to draw up really accurate maps of much of the interior. The actual copying of maps in the forward area was first done by photographic means, but the lenses of the day introduced a degree of distortion so that it proved difficult, if not impossible, to match the edges of two adjacent map sheets accurately. The correct procedure was to engrave the maps and then reproduce them by lithography, but the equipment for this was far too bulky to be carted around behind the survey parties, and it demanded far too many draftsmen and printers to be a practical proposition. Lithography was therefore carried out well behind the lines, using the sketch maps and survey notes prepared by field parties. For quick provision to the field armies, a chemical system similar to that used for making engineer's blueprints was employed. The map was drawn, again from survey notes and sketches, on a thin paper sheet. This was then stretched over a sheet sensitized by soaking in a silver nitrate solution and the two were exposed to sunlight. Where the light passed through the paper unimpeded, the lower sheet turned black; where the lines on the top sheet stopped the light, the lower sheet remained white. The lower sheet was then chemically 'fixed' and the result was a map of white lines on a black background. Due to the fugitive nature of the chemical process, these maps soon faded, but they could be easily replaced and, since they were temporary maps, their lack of permanence was not important. They sufficed for the immediate needs of a battle, and were in due course replaced by the more elegant and durable maps prepared by the lithographers.

The Topographic Engineers were also responsible for reconnaissance of routes, both from the mapping point of view and also from that of assessing the resources of an area which could be turned to use by the advancing army. Thus in addition to providing the general with a sketch map of a route, the engineers would report on the strength and location of bridges, the nature of roads and railroads, the provision of such things as corn and water mills, sawmills, timber, buildings suitable for headquarters, river crossings and fords and virtually anything else which might be of value.

The Union Army was well provided with engineers. It had the nucleus of its force in the regular army corps which were all in Union territory at the outbreak of war, and these were soon expanded. The necessary officer strength was

Below: Men of the 7th Pennsylvania Regiment at work manufacturing fascines (bundles of sticks) and gabions (baskets to be filled with rocks and dirt) for field fortifications and breastworks.

found from men with engineering training, of which there was a sufficient supply, and the men were easily trained to the relatively simple duties of field engineers. The complex equipment of today's engineers was unknown, of course; most engineering tasks were competently performed with nothing more complex than picks and shovels, and the ability to use these was commonplace at that time. In addition to their engineer function, though, the corps were soldiers and were therefore trained in the basic skills of an infantryman; which was just as well, for there were many cases where they had to throw their shovels aside and take to their rifles and muskets.

The Confederates were less well off. They had very few engineer officers, and most of the engineer posts had to be filled by civil engineers. The principal difference was that the Confederates had, at first, no Corps of Engineers. They relied upon their Pioneer Corps, which was brought to strength by simply transferring infantry from different brigades and placing them under the control of the qualified engineers. On occasion, even Pioneer Corps men were not available, and more than one Confederate engineering problem was solved by sending out the Provost Corps to round up any unoccupied male, civil or military, in the area and impress him into doing what was necessary under armed guard. This system was obviously inadequate, and in 1863 two Confederate Engineer Regiments were formed, each of 10 companies of 100 men.

The primary role of the Corps of Engineers, fortification, had occupied them continuously since their foundation early in the century, and as a result there were a large number of powerful forts distributed down the Atlantic seaboard for coast defense purposes. The war was to demonstrate that these works had now been overtaken by the development of artillery, and there were to be far-reaching changes in the science of fortification as a result of the Civil War.

The construction of fortifications was more or less based on classical principles which had been developed in Europe over the centuries, modified from time to time as experience dictated. As a result of this, the pre-war American forts were large brick and masonry structures, generally pentagonal but occasionally with protruding bastions, and sometimes with two or three floors of guns so as to present an approaching fleet with an overpowering weight of artillery. While presenting an enormous target, they relied for their survival on the simple fact that they could overpower an enemy fleet before that fleet could get close enough to do any damage. A ship was not a steady

Below: The siege of Vicksburg, July 1863, under General Grant, showing the use of gabions to provide breastworks and cover for the advancing lines.

Above: Fort Walker, Hilton Head, Port Royal Harbor, under attack by a Union fleet, 7 November 1861. This shows the general layout of a fort of the period; note how large mounds or 'traverses' behind the guns protect the gunners from the effects of any explosive shells landing inside the fort.

Top right: Carrying gunpowder to charge a subterranean mine excavated by Union troops during the siege of Petersburg, 1864.

Lower right: Field defenses around Petersburg.

firing platform, and successive shots from a ship-mounted gun would never impact in the same place, so that the effect of shipborne guns would be distributed and thus reduced. On the other hand the fortress artillery, firmly emplaced and behind protection, could generally produce accurate and concentrated fire to damage ships at long range.

The remainder of these works were also in conformity with the accepted practices of the day They were surrounded by deep ditches containing water, the outer side of which presented a smooth 'glacis' facing the land side and across which attacking troops would have to expose themselves to the fire of guns on top of the fort walls and concealed in casemates inside the work. Land approaches were often additionally fortified by outworks, and the interior of the fort was provided with barracks and stores which were protected from mortar attack by thick layers of earth. They were generally considered to be impregnable.

The events of the Civil War upset these calculations, since when either side attacked these coastal forts they did not do so from ships but by bringing field and siege artillery overland to attack the fort either from the rear or flank, or frontally, across a narrow stretch of water. Fort Pulaski, near the mouth of the Savannah River, was occupied by state troops in January 1861, three months before the war began. It was retaken some 15 months later by Union troops who brought up siege artillery and bombarded from long range. Instead of the smooth-bore cannon which the fort had been designed to resist, the Union troops produced rifled artillery of considerable power, and they very soon breached the masonry. More than any other single event, the breaching of Fort Pulaski finally established rifled artillery as the masters of masonry works, and led to a complete change in the nature of fortifications. Henceforth even formal fortification would have more in common with field works; earth ramparts, it was realized, were a better protection against the fire of rifled guns since they smothered the arriving shell rather than presenting a hard vertical face guaranteed to detonate it or to offer an ideal target to pointed shot.

Field fortifications, which sprang up all over the battle zone, ranged from simple trenches scraped by soldiers with bayonet and shovel to extremely involved complexes of trenches and gun batteries. They generally began as trenches, and were then gradually improved by the addition of revetments, to prevent the sides of the trenches collapsing, dug-out shelters to protect off-duty soldiers, prepared platforms for heavy artillery, listening posts, sentry posts, observation posts and communication trenches, all protected by thick ramparts of sandbags or earth-filled log walls. Sixty-eight such minor forts surrounded

Washington, all connected by some 20 miles of trenches; three independent rings of works surrounded Richmond, and the final line of works protecting the Richmond-Petersburg complex was larger even than the Washington defenses.

To assault these types of work involved more than merely assembling troops and rushing them. The works were laid out with care by the Engineer Corps so that fields of fire interlocked; obstacles such as *trous-de-loup* (holes in the ground with sharpened stakes at the bottom), *chevaux-de-frise* (logs pierced by sharpened and fire-hardened stakes) and *abattis* (trees felled and trimmed so as to present a tangle of sharpened branches to the enemy) were employed in profusion. Land mines might be laid, generally consisting of artillery shells or mortar bombs with simple percussion fuzes, so placed that they might be stepped on by advancing troops. And in the rear would be artillery aimed at specific lines of approach so as to decimate the attack with spherical case shot before it got within musket range of the defenders. None of this was going to be taken by mere dash and bravado.

The approved method of assaulting prepared defenses was one which dated from the seven-

Above: The siege of Vicksburg; a line of riflemen protected by gabions, with a pit giving cover for off-duty troops.

teenth century and which was to survive the Civil War to see its final employment in the twentieth century: the method known in brief as 'sap and parallel'. The assaulting force first laid out its lines, well clear of the defenses, installing siege artillery and mortars in well-dug pits which afforded protection. From this line, trenches – known as 'saps' – were excavated forward, toward the defenses. They ran in zigzag manner, so that it was not possible for a defender to fire down the length of a sap. This excavation was fraught with danger, since the defenders knew precisely what was happening and were trying to prevent it; therefore the front end of the sap was generally protected by some sort of shield, pushed forward on rollers, to protect the diggers.

About halfway to the defended line, a connecting line of trench would be excavated, linking up all the saps; this was the 'parallel', since it was parallel to the defense work. Both saps and parallel would now be enlarged until it was possible to use the saps to bring forward artillery and mortars and establish more siege batteries closer to the objective. Then fresh saps would be begun, ending fairly close to the defense works in a 'second parallel'.

From this line, new saps would go forward. Some of these would be directed at the part of the defenses which the attackers had decided was the weakest point and one which could be profitably attacked. Others would be directed toward other specific points, the object being to keep the defenders guessing as to where the eventual attack would be made.

While all this excavation was going forward the siege batteries would have kept up a constant bombardment of the defenses, aiming firstly at general destruction and keeping the enemy occupied, and secondly at breaching the defenses by smashing down some selected objectives, one of which would be the target of the final saps.

Finally, and usually at night, troops would be fed forward down the saps and parallels to the selected area of attack, and from the end of the sap the assaulting party would leap out and head for the 'breach', that section of the defensive structure which by now would have been collapsed by the fire of the siege batteries. If the whole affair had been conducted properly, the assault would take the breach, expand it and feed the remainder of the troops through it and into the objective.

In the classic days of European fortress warfare, the actual assault rarely took place; the breach was made by artillery, the sap was there for the defenders to see, and the next move was staringly obvious. The commander of the besieged place was now invited to surrender, since a 'practicable breach' had been made, and it was obvious that the subsequent battle was going to be both bloody and unnecessary. Surrender was usually given after some gentlemanly haggling over terms, and that was that.

In the Civil War this attitude did not exist. Nobody was going to surrender, and anybody who wanted to take the defended place was going to have to do it the hard way. The few times when this tactic was employed resulted in grim and bloody hand-to-hand fighting before either the work was subdued or the attackers repulsed.

On campaign, the engineer's task was to facilitate the advance of the army by overcoming

Right: The siege of Vicksburg; the fighting in the crater on Fort Hill after the explosion of a Union mine, 25 June 1863.

obstacles. This could mean anything from improving the surface of a road to laying bridges to demolishing enemy field defenses after their capture so as to prevent their reuse. For most of the time his work was simple civil engineering, making 'corduroy' roads by laying timber down on earth roads so as to give an all-weather surface, cutting new roads and tracks where necessary, and bridging rivers and streams.

The theater of war was criss-crossed by innumerable rivers and streams, and the paucity of roads in those days meant that bridges were relatively few. It was impossible for advancing armies, which were bound by the tactical facts of the enemy's presence, to select their route so that it coincided with the existing bridges, and, of course, the retreating army generally made sure that any bridges it left behind were destroyed or at least severely damaged. Thus bridging became one of the major engineer tasks on both sides. Every corps had its bridging train, thirty or forty wagons carrying specialist equipment, and this

Right: An excellent example of formal fortification techniques. Notice the earth traverse, reinforced with gabions, between the gun emplacements, the embrasures for the gun muzzles, and the protected position for ammunition behind the traverse.

Above: Pontoon Waggon Bridge Train Number 104 on the march from Aquia Creek to the Rappahannock River.

was never far behind the leading troops of the advance, ready to be called forward to deal with the next water crossing.

The bridging trains were based on French and Russian originals. The most involved system was the wooden pontoon, taken from a French Army pattern; this consisted of a heavy flat-bottomed and square-ended wooden boat carried on a massive four-wheeled wagon. On arrival at the river edge, the pontoon was manhandled off the wagon and slid into the water, then anchored in line with the stream. The next pontoon was launched and poled and paddled into place alongside the first, then securely lashed. More pontoons followed until, eventually, the final one was maneuvered into place alongside the opposite bank, making a bridge of boats across the water.

Now the 'chess wagons' and 'balk wagons' were brought to the bridge site and unloaded. The 'balks' were 27-foot-long, five-inch square timbers which were now carried and laid across the tops of the pontoons, five lines of balks being

laid and lashed into place. Finally, on top of the balks, the 'chesses', 13-foot planks, were laid crossways to form the treadway of the bridge. With these secured in place the pontoon bridge was ready for use. In practice, of course, the whole construction would have moved in a more compact manner; the balks would have started to go down as soon as two or three pontoons had been anchored, and the chesses would follow, so that by the time the final pontoon was placed in position, the deck of the bridge would be only a few feet behind it. The chesses were often covered with a layer of straw or earth in order to protect the timber from the chipping to be expected from hooves and iron-shod wheels.

An alternative, and lighter, form of pontoon was copied from a Russian Army pattern. This was simply an open framework of wood, rectangular in form, which was built up from pre-cut and pre-jointed sections on top of a large sheet of canvas about 35 feet long and 10 feet wide. The framework was 26 feet long, 5.5 feet wide and 2.5 feet deep, and once it had been built the edges of the canvas were pulled up, around the sides of the frame, and secured with ropes so as to form a canvas pontoon. This could be used in exactly the same way as the wooden pontoon, but was generally restricted to marching troops and the lighter forms of horse-drawn traffic. It had the advantage of being less heavy and bulky and requiring fewer wagons to carry the components.

In addition to these prefabricated pontoon systems (which were scarce in the Confederate Army) the engineers and pioneers were experts at throwing together rafts from whatever they could find in the vicinity. Some Union engineer units were supplied with inflatable canvas and rubber pontoons, formed of three cylinders making a unit some 20 feet long and five feet wide, and these could be used either as a basis for rafts or as pontoons for a light footbridge.

Above: Field engineering is not without hazards; at the Battle of Fredericksburg the engineers poled across the river in pontoon boats in order to clear out Confederate sharpshooters interfering with their bridge construction.

Right: A Union pontoon bridge. Note the dirt and straw laid on the deck to protect the surface from damage by horseshoes.

Various examples of pontoon bridges; the main picture is a bridge laid from Georgetown DC across the Potomac to the Virginia shore.

The Medical Services

At the outbreak of war the US Army Medical Department mustered just 115 officers and men. Of these, 27 resigned, 24 of them going to the South to form the Confederate Medical Department. Bearing in mind that the two sides had placed more than two million men under arms by the end of the war, it is obvious that an immense medical staff had to be conjured up from somewhere and equipped to deal with the casualties which might be expected. More than that, medical staffs were vital to try to protect the army from the consequences of disease, since at that time it was still expected that more would die or fall ill from disease in the field than would actually succumb to enemy action. The total casualties sustained by the two sides in the Civil War are not accurately known; but we do know that at Antietam, for example, the Union sustained 12,400 casualties and the Confederates 13,700 – and Antietam has been called 'the bloodiest one-day battle of the entire war'. In the one-month period covering Cold Harbor, The Wilderness and Spotsylvania, the Union sustained 54,929 casualties – 52 percent of its troops – while the Confederates took losses of 39,000 – 59 percent of its troops. Overall, Southern losses have been estimated at 442,000 and Union losses at 360,000. Of these about two-thirds died of disease.

This was nothing unusual at that time; knowledge of the causes of disease was scanty, and where the causes were unknown it is not surprising that remedies were generally ineffective. Personal hygiene was poor by modern standards, as was sanitation generally, and confining hundreds, sometimes thousands, of men in close proximity established some very favorable conditions for disease to spread. There was also, according to some contemporary statements, a degree of 'emancipation' among many of the younger soldiers; they had volunteered for the Army to get away from the restrictions of home life, and among those restrictions were such tiresome demands as washing and changing clothes from time to time. Add to this bad weather, foul water, poor food and poor physical condition, and the results were inevitable.

The solution to much of this was discipline, but discipline was not a popular concept in the early days of the war. Regular Army units had discipline and attended to their sanitary require-

Below: A field dressing station at the battle of Antietam, with wounded being removed to hospital by ambulance wagon after temporary treatment.

Right: The Battle of Antietam, 17 September 1862, when over 26,000 men fell in a single day, the most appalling and concentrated carnage of the entire war.

ments with routine application. But discipline was not required by volunteers; they had enlisted to shoot the enemy, not to fool around calling people 'sir' and obeying orders they considered to be pointless. It took some time and some shuffling of incompetent officers before the need for discipline could be driven into the volunteers; once this happened, once they began to see that obedience to a few simple orders was likely to save their lives, things began to improve. But even so, disease was never absent from the ranks of either army.

At the start of the war the Union Army's arrangements for dealing with battle casualties can best be described as haphazard. Ambulances were the responsibility of the Quartermaster

Right: Union Ambulance Corps collecting wounded after a battle.

Corps and were generally impressed wagons driven by civilian drivers, whose willingness to serve got less as they approached the scene of battle. Collection of the wounded from the field was, as with most armies, the responsibility of the regimental band who doubled as stretcher-bearers in time of war. They, being few, were aided by whatever men the unit commander felt he could spare; since these were generally the men he felt he could get along without, their application to duty was not of the highest, and a wounded man might very well lie out in the field for hours or even days before being found and carried to safety. Once brought in, he would be given elementary first-aid attention in the regimental aid post and then transferred to an ambulance cart for transportation to a hospital. This, it appears, is where the organization began to falter, since the ambulance carts might not appear; their drivers might have thought better of it, or their horses might have been commandeered to pull guns or furnish remounts for cavalry.

After some appalling reports of the treatment of casualties during the first battles, McClellan was moved to make some organizational changes. He removed the ambulance responsibility from the Quartermaster Corps and set up an independent Federal Ambulance Corps which, as well as providing ambulances and their staff, also undertook the supply of medical stores to hospitals and aid posts. The chain of casualty evacuation was also rationalized. The wounded man was taken to a regimental aid station for immediate aid; then he was placed in an ambulance and back-loaded to the divisional field hospital, sufficiently far behind the lines to be out of danger from enemy artillery. Here major surgery took place on those who required it, while minor in-

Below: Inside a railroad hospital car moving wounded back from the war zone to base hospitals.

Above: Wounded troops arriving by train at Stevenson, Alabama, after the Battle of Chickamauga.

juries were nursed back to health. More serious casualties, after surgery and brief rest, would be moved again, to larger base and general hospitals in the rear area, either by ambulance or, more usually, by hospital train.

The divisional hospital was set up in a cluster of about twenty tents and was deemed sufficient to cope with the casualties from a combat group 8000 strong. The regimental hospitals, which were a feature of the early system, were disbanded, their staff and equipment being assimilated into the divisional organization. One advantage of this was that it removed a somewhat unfortunate parochialism under which surgeons were often reluctant to deal with soldiers from another regiment who might have been delivered to their hospital.

The base hospitals grew to enormous sizes. Chimborazo Hospital, close to Richmond, was at one time the world's largest medical establishment, capable of holding almost 5000 patients at one time and incorporating its own farm and bakery to supply a wholesome diet to them.

The ambulances were generally sprung light wagons, which gave a moderately comfortable ride to their patients. In the Confederate states their small stock of sprung wagons rapidly fell to pieces with overuse, and the Army had to fall back on ordinary country carts and wagons unless they were fortunate enough to capture some Union ambulances. Hospital trains, at first, were no more than trains of empty boxcars provided with straw upon which to lay the litters, but these were gradually improved. Regular railroad day coaches were rebuilt with bunks, while special cars fitted as dispensaries and emergency surgeries, kitchens and accommodation for the medical staff were attached to attend to the patients' welfare during the trip.

The medical staff were a mixed lot. The Union Army's regular establishment remained almost what it had been at the outbreak of war, and it was augmented by intakes of Regimental Surgeons and Assistant Surgeons who accompanied the formation of volunteer regiments. Like the officers of these regiments, the surgeons were state appointees and were of very mixed quality. At best they were excellent doctors who gave up their civil practice to do their best for the soldiers. At worst they were ignorant leeches with dubious qualifications. Supervision by the Medical Department of the Army gradually weeded out the worst cases, but such weeding was reluctant, since the supply of surgeons never matched the demand.

The nursing staff of the hospitals were invariably men, except in base hospitals where a limited number of female nurses was tolerated. There was still considerable prejudice among the military against female nurses, but this was gradually being overcome and the number of females perceptibly increased as the war progressed. The nursing staff were also augmented by patients who were convalescing; once a patient was able to move about he was generally found some job to occupy him and take some of the work from the shoulders of the regular staff.

In addition to the Medical Department, the Union also had the services of the US Sanitary Commission. This quasi-official body had been set up in 1861 in order to supplement the regular medical organization, and it gradually became a powerful and respected body. It oversaw the sanitary arrangements of camps, provided medical assistance, supplied medical necessities to regiments and divisional hospitals, and accompanied armies in the field as a sort of combined welfare and health organization. It ran hospital boats on the rivers, to move men back to base hospitals, organized convalescent homes to relieve the burden on army hospitals, and even supervised the distribution of gifts of food and clothing from various patriotic funds.

Rations

By the standards of the day the authorized ration of the soldier of the Civil War was reasonable, if not luxurious. The Union soldier in camp was allowed 12 ounces of pork (usually in the form of bacon or ham) or 20 ounces of salt or fresh beef; one pound of hard bread; four ounces of dried peas or beans; two ounces of rice or hominy grits; one and a quarter ounces of ground roast coffee – rather more if issued as green beans; two ounces of sugar; four ounces of potatoes; and a sufficiency of salt, pepper, vinegar and molasses.

By comparison, the Confederate soldier was rather worse off. His allowance amounted to eight ounces of meat, 18 ounces of flour, about three ounces of peas or beans, an ounce of sugar and some salt.

Both of these rations would be augmented, as the season and situation permitted, by local purchases of fresh fruit and vegetables, and the Union Army also pioneered the development of such novelties as dehydrated vegetables and a form of instant coffee – a paste of finely ground coffee, sugar and skim milk.

But the fact of the matter was that this 'authorized' ration, was not necessarily what the soldier actually got, situated as he might be at the end of a long and tenuous supply line. The meat, for example, would more often than not be substandard beef pickled in brine. It was common to throw the barrel in a running stream and leave it overnight in the hope of leaching out the salt so that by morning the meat would be slightly more palatable. Unfortunately this also leached out much of the content of the meat as well, and removing the overpowering taste of salt generally revealed that the meat had been far from its best when it was preserved. Scandals over tainted meat being sold to the armies by rascally contractors were nothing new, nor did they end with the Civil War – the same complaints were being heard 30 years later in the Spanish-American War and 30 years after that in World War One.

Likewise, the bread would rarely be a leavened loaf of soft bread; it was more likely to be 'hardtack', the unleavened flour-and-water biscuit, about three inches square and half an inch thick. These also depended upon the individual contractor for their quality, some tasting better than

Right: This idyllic scene of camp life was probably at odds with reality, but doubtless attracted recruits and reassured relatives at home.

Above: Augmenting the rations: Confederate guerrillas capture a Union supply train.

others, but all were as hard as bricks and frequently riddled with weevils; the Civil War soldier soon adopted the old-time sailor's trick of banging his biscuit on a hard surface in order to persuade most of the inmates to wriggle out before beginning to eat.

Hardtack could be made more palatable by softening and flavoring it. At the least, this meant dunking it in coffee, a fairly commonplace practice. More complex methods involved breaking up the biscuit and using it as an ingredient for a simple stew, boiling salt beef, bacon, hardtack

Above: A sutler's store at Harper's Ferry, doubtless the first drive-in store. The bottle of gin on the shelf belies the 'no alcohol' regulation.

and whatever vegetables were available together in a messkit. Another variant was to crumble the biscuit and fry it in pork fat.

Milk was rarely seen in its fresh condition, and condensed milk was the general issue – when it was available.

Once on campaign the ration became more sparse. The Union 'marching ration' was one pound of hardtack, 12 ounces of salt or 20 ounces of fresh meat, sugar, coffee and salt. This was issued to the individual, and it was up to him how, or if, he cooked it. At the end of the day he would, if the weather and tactical conditions permitted, light a small fire and do what he could to make the ration more palatable, perhaps frying the meat or making some sort of a stew. But if the conditions did not permit a fire, he would simply eat what he had in its raw state.

As might be expected, good old American enterprise came to the assistance of the individual soldiers; on the line of march they would industriously forage for anything eatable. Like all front line soldiers they had no compunction about 'liberating' anything that came their way which might add to the day's ration, and they had no truck with anyone who considered such actions as looting. Looting was something entirely different – that was simply theft for personal gain; foraging was respectable, being no more than insurance against hunger in conditions where the next meal was problematic. Moreover, men who would never dream of stealing valuables from a fallen comrade would, without hesitation, empty his ration haversack to supplement their own. But as the war progressed, the opportunity to gain anything from foraging became less and less; as the theater of war was marched and counter-marched by numerous hungry troops, so the edible produce of the countryside grew more scarce.

The basic issue ration was sufficient to keep a man alive – it has officially been reckoned at something in the order of 2500 calories – but it was low on vitamins and the lack of green stuffs frequently caused outbreaks of scurvy among units. In order to improve the ration, even at the individual's own expense, each regiment permitted a 'sutler' to accompany them on campaign. The sutler was a private operator who followed the regiment with a wagon and, at the end of the day's march, would set up his booth in the bivouac area to sell tobacco, fruit, candy, soft drinks, sugar and whatever other food he could lay in, plus such requisites as writing paper, razors, newspapers, books and knives. In a word, he was the Civil War equivalent of today's Post Exchange. His prices were regulated by a board of officers, and his stock was inspected and regulated by the Inspector General's Department in order to ensure that he sold articles of reasonable quality at a reasonable price. He was forbidden to sell liquor, and any infraction of this rule was followed by instant expulsion, but the regulations as to price and quality were less well enforced, and in more than one regiment the dissatisfied soldiers took matters into their own hands when confronted with a profiteering sutler.

The Quartermaster's Department

The Quartermaster's Department, in both armies, was responsible for supplying the field forces with whatever common-user items they required. This means that, for example, the supply of bridging equipment to the engineers was an engineer responsibility, but the supply of uniforms, rations, tents or shovels to the engineers came under the Quartermaster's organization, since these items were needed by the entire army and it made sense to have their supply attended to by one source. Rations were kept separate from the remainder of the supply system, and were dealt with by a Commissary Department; they were obtained from contractors and distributed by the Department through its own echelons down to divisions, brigades and regiments, each formation having its own Commissary representatives.

The actual task of distributing the multitude of other stores was undertaken by wagon trains run by the Quartermaster Corps and also by railroad trains allocated by the Military Railroad Service to the QMC. Railroad distribution was largely done to a number of major railhead dumps, from which the wagon trains set out to find the armies in the field. Such wagon trains became a considerable problem; a regiment of 1000 men could well have a permanent train of 30 wagons doing nothing but shuttle back and forth between regiment and railhead keeping the supplies flowing. Multiply this by the number of regiments in an army, and some idea of the problem begins to appear. McClellan, in the Peninsula, had 5000 wagons in his Quartermaster trains, and the task of ensuring that the forward flow of laden wagons was not interrupted by the rearward flow of empties meant careful planning of routes and adherence to fairly precise timetables. To add to the confusion, supply trains had a lower priority than either marching troops or artillery columns, and the presence of either on a planned route soon played havoc with all the schedules. Bear in mind also that in the 1860s the actual number of roads and bridges was far less than it is today, and the roads themselves were not sealed blacktop but rough, stony earth, which rapidly turned into sticky mud under the pounding of hooves and wheels in any rainstorm.

Of all the various items delivered by the Quartermasters, perhaps the one in which the soldier took most interest was clothing, since much of the issue clothing soon wore out and replacement became a vital matter. In the early part of the war, when uniforms were desperately needed and contractors were given orders without very care-

Below: A rare photograph, from a cracked glass negative, of the 3rd Cavalry Division ammunition train near Brandy Station, Virginia, in 1864.

Right: Disaster on the supply route as a store wagon and its train of mules leaves a bridge while crossing Kettle Run.

ful examination of their samples, some appalling rubbish reached the troops. Union and Confederate alike were issued with clothing made from 'shoddy', a material woven from reused wool, the clippings from carpets and the scraps from tailors' shops. This made a short-fiber cloth which looked quite sound and was satisfactory so long as it remained dry, but as soon as it got wet – as it inevitably did on campaign – the short weave simply fell to pieces. As soon as this became obvious the War Departments and Quartermaster Corps moved on the contractors to ensure that

Right: And more disaster as Confederate guerrillas snipe at a Union supply column on the Tennessee River.

Above: Supply wagons in reserve at Yorktown, part of the enormous resources required by McClellan's force in the Peninsula.

outer clothing was made from first-use wool with long fibers, but the profit margin on shoddy was too good to forgo, and the contractors continued to use it wherever they could get away with it.

The two armies are always celebrated as the Blues and the Grays, reflecting the color of their dress uniforms. The Union soldier was provided with a dress hat, dark blue frock coat or jacket, dark blue trousers, and a fatigue blouse and cap for day-to-day wear. Over his left shoulder went a cartridge box on a strap, and around his waist was a belt carrying a bayonet and a box for percussion caps. On his right shoulder was his ration haversack and water canteen. On his back was an oiled-cloth knapsack, around which was bound a shelter half and a blanket. Inside the knapsack would be his spare clothing – two shirts, two pairs of drawers, dress coat and hat. He would also have a greatcoat, tin plate, cutlery, towel and soap and whatever personal belongings he chose to carry – which was rarely very much.

The Confederate soldier's outfit was very similar, though often his uniform was a wool and cotton mixture cloth which was lighter than that of the Union soldier and probably more comfortable in the heat of summer. The coloring, though, was rarely a uniform gray; it ran from a very dark shade to a near-brown, a color which was due to the Southern practice of dyeing the cloth with a mixture of butternut oil and iron sulphate. Depending, therefore, on the dye content of the oil, the texture of the cloth and the dyeing technique employed, the actual color could range through a broad cast of shades which, according to one report, ran from 'deep coffee brown up to the whitish brown of ordinary dust'. The Confederate Army was, of course, hampered in its production of cloth by the blockade, since it did not have such extensive woolen manufactories as the North, and therefore had to make do with whatever cloth and dye it could manage to acquire. Toward the end of the war, and certainly from the latter part of 1864, the supply of dye was at least regularized and from then on the official gray shade became standard.

For a marching army boots were of vital importance, and their supply was a constant problem. Union troops were issued with black leather 'Jefferson shoes', a high-sided shoe of generous width and square-cut shape with a low heel. A

Above: The 5th Vermont Regiment at Camp Griffin, Virginia, in 1861.

pair of these, of good quality, could be expected to last for a couple of months; if they were of poor quality they would not survive one rainstorm. These shoes were generally made with the rough side of the leather to the outside and the soles could be sewn or pegged to the uppers. In all, some two and a half million pairs of shoes were procured by the Union Army during the war, and each man was authorized four pairs a year, but in many cases the individual soldier had to resort to the sutler and buy a pair of shoes in default of his regular issue. Cavalrymen wore mid-calf length boots, generally of better quality than the foot-soldier's shoes and lasting longer since the horse soldier rarely walked when he could ride.

Confederate soldiers wore the same pattern of Jefferson shoe, either locally made or imported; in either case the quality was generally worse than

Right: A Union Army blacksmith and his field forge outside Petersburg, August 1864. Notice the portable bellows and forge.

Right: A Union Army wagon repair depot, with wheelwrights at work, February 1864.

that of the Union products, the leather often being poorly tanned and thus less durable.

These briefly outlined details were the regulation standard; but in actual practice there were so many deviations from standard that the uniforms of the Civil War are a study in themselves, and one into which we cannot go deeply. The first cause for deviation was the individuality of state militia and volunteer regiments, which often adopted their own dress embellishments and, in many cases, adopted uniforms which were totally different from those laid down in regulations for the Army. The most prominent of these variants were the 'Zouave' uniforms affected by several regiments in both the Union and Confederate Armies, though those of the Union were more numerous. Just what caused this craze for the outlandish Zouave uniform, copied from that of the French Algerian troops, is unclear, but the short jackets, baggy trousers, waist-sash, fez-style headgear and ornate decorations were immensely popular, particularly with regiments from the Eastern states, though one or two Texas regiments also adopted the style. In 1864 the US Army actually authorized and issued Zouave uniforms to one or two regiments as a mark of distinction for proficiency. Other regiments with non-standard uniforms included Berdan's Sharpshooters, who wore dark green clothing with black buttons, doubtless in emulation of the British Army's rifle regiments, and the 'Garibaldi Guards' or 39th New York Infantry, who adopted a dark blue-green uniform and a wide-brimmed hat carrying a plume of feathers. Most of these ornate uniforms lasted in service until they wore out, after which the regiments reverted to the regulation style of their particular army, but one or two Northern Zouave regiments managed to maintain the supply, by importing from France, throughout the war.

The second reason for deviation from the regulation dress was simply the difficulty of replacing it during a campaign. This was particularly the case with the Confederate troops as the war went into its second half. By that time the clothing shortages were beginning to be felt, and the transportation and supply situation was also deteriorating. As a result the Confederate soldier dressed himself in whatever came to hand, even to the extent of stripping Union bodies on the battlefield for their clothing. The Confederate commanders tried to stamp out this practice, without success; 'Yankee overcoats' were much prized.

Another defect in the Confederate system was that each state looked after its own regiments as best it could, but only its own regiments. Instead of regarding their output of clothing as being for the benefit of the Army as a whole, parochialism ruled; in the last winter of the war the Governor of North Carolina held 92,000 sets of clothing and blankets in his warehouses but refused to allow them to be issued for the benefit of Lee's army, by then suffering the rigors of winter. The clothing was surplus to the needs of the North Carolina troops, but nevertheless it stayed in store rather than be issued to any of the ill-clad out-of-state regiments.

INDEX

Page numbers in *italics* refer to illustrations

Picture Credits

BBC Hulton Picture Library: pages 61, 64-65, 68 (bottom), 84

Bison Picture Library: pages 3, 6-7, 11, 17, 114-5, 118 (top), 136 (top), 137 (bottom), 144 (top), 153, 166

Anne SK Brown Military Collection, Brown University: pages 66, 67 (both), 79 (both), 85, 86 (bottom), 89 (bottom), 91 (bottom), 157 (top), 158, 161 (top right), 163 (top)

Chicago Historical Society: pages 62-63, 81 (bottom), 120-121

Christies East, New York: pages 18, 20 (bottom), 42 (bottom)

Department of the Environment, UK: page 42 (top)

DuPont De Nemours & Co (from collection in the Remington Museum): pages 22 (bottom), 27 (top), 28 (top), 46 (bottom)

Ian Hogg: pages 24 (both), 26 (top), 27 (bottom), 28 (bottom), 29 (top), 53, 54, 55, 68 (top), 69 (top), 73, 76 (both), 86 (top), 87, 94, 95, 112, 113 (top), 139, 140 (both), 146 (top), 151, 159 (bottom)

Library of Congress: pages 4-5, 8, 9, 32-33, 40-1, 44-5, 48-9, 56, 58-9, 60, 69 (bottom), 72, 77, 82, 83, 88, 92, 97, 124, 137 (top), 142, 148-9, 150, 155 (bottom), 157 (bottom), 160-1, 169, 171, 172 (top)

Museum of the Confederacy: pages 122, 126 (top), 147

National Park Service, Springfield Armory National Historic Site: pages 12, 13, 16, 35 (both), 37 (both), 38 (top), 43 (bottom), 51, 52

New York Public Library: page 81 (top)

Peter Newark's Western Americana: pages 10, 15 (top), 19 (both), 20 (top), 21 (both), 23, 26 (bottom), 29 (bottom), 30-31, 34, 37, 38 (bottom), 39 (both), 43 (top), 46 (top), 47, 50 (both), 54 (top), 57, 70 (both), 71 (both), 80, 89 (top), 90, 95 (top), 102, 103, 105, 107, 108-9, 110 (top), 111, 116, 117, 118 (bottom), 119 (both), 123, 125 (both), 126 (bottom), 127 (both), 128, 129, 130, 131, 132-3, 134, 135, 136 (bottom), 138 (both), 141, 143, 144 (bottom), 145 (both), 152, 155 (top), 156, 159 (top), 160 (top left), 162, 163 (bottom), 164, 165, 167, 168, 170 (both), 172 (bottom), 173

Courtesy of The Royal Artillery Institution (Museum of Artillery at the Rotunda), London (Photos Joseph Coughlan): pages 14 (all 3) 15 (bottom 3), 22 (top), 36 (both), 74, 75 (both), 98, 99

Beverley R Robinson Collection, US Naval Academy Museum: page 104

Rutherford B Hayes/Presidential Center: page 1

Smith & Wesson: page 25

US Naval Historical Center: pages 106, 110 (bottom), 113 (bottom), 154

Virginia State Library: pages 100-1